SECRETS
— OF —
MINISTERIAL
SUCCESS
Advice to My Students

GARY S. MAXEY

Introduction by Prof. E. M. Uka

SECRETS OF MINISTERIAL SUCCESS

Advice to My Students

Published by

 West Africa Theological Seminary
36 Olukunle Akinola Street
Ipaja, Lagos, NIGERIA

ISBN: 9798676300050

Contact Addresses:
Gary S. Maxey, Founder, WATS, PMB 003, Ipaja, Lagos
Email: drgarymaxey@gmail.com; Tel: +234-808-726-6310

Designed and Printed by:
asbotgraphics

OTHER BOOKS BY GARY S. MAXEY

The WATS Journey: A Personal Narrative

New Life in Christ

New Life in Christ, Yoruba

Capturing a Lost Vision: Can Nigeria's
Greatest Revival Live Again?

The Seduction of the Nigerian Church

Discovering the New Testament

Discovering the Old Testament

Confessions of a Grateful Pilgrim

The Highway of Holiness

Standing Firm in Christ

The Thessalonian Road: Sanctification Made Plain

Living Nigeria on Purpose, Vol. 1 – 4

Juju vs. Christianity: An African Dilemma

Going Deeper with God

Our Great God

Our Great Salvation

Why the Nigerian Revival Tarries

Escaping Sexual Bondage:
Moral Purity in a Hostile World

The Spirit World

Contents

Introduction

Dr. Gary Maxey speaks from his heart in this book, giving us his understanding of what is required to succeed in Christian ministry. My personal view is that this book should be considered part of a trilogy of books he has produced, all of which discuss the health of the Nigerian Church.

The first book is *The Seduction of the Nigerian Church*, in which he critically reflects on the corruption of the church from her fundamental biblical principles. In that book he and his co-author, Dr. Peter Ozodo, outline four areas in which the Nigerian Church has been lured away from its foundations. The unbalanced Prosperity Gospel, the infiltration of the spirit and practices of African Traditional Religion, the loss of a sound understanding of spirituality, and capitulation to the Hyper-Grace movement are all highlighted.

The second book in Dr. Maxey's trilogy is *Why the Nigerian Revival Tarries.* This book deals with human failures that have delayed revival in the Nigerian Church. In many cases, church leaders have side-tracked biblical revival, which Dr. Maxey defines as "a spontaneous spiritual awakening by the Holy Spirit among professing Christians that is preceded by a deepened spiritual experience, holy living, evangelism, and missions." Regrettably, church leaders have often turned worship into a time of celebrating what the author calls "cheap triumphalism." That is the compulsive idea that "all is well" and that everybody is happy. By this means worship in the house of God becomes an emotionally gratifying experience, wherein we demand entertainment and pleasure. All we want to hear is "Tonight your problems will end," or "Tonight you will not go home with your problems." This kind of irresponsible proclamation almost always short circuits the work of the Holy Spirit. It is a revival killer.

The third book is this present volume, *Secrets of Ministerial Success: Advice to my Students.* This book provides fundamental biblical principles that can help ministers of the Gospel overcome their failures to ignite the long-awaited revival of the Nigerian Church. Here Dr. Maxey puts forth the principles by which the Nigerian Church could be revived through the instrumentality of born-again Nigerian ministers, who would in turn influence their members.

With amazing clarity and pastoral insight, the author identifies thirteen secrets that he believes are necessary to achieve ministerial success. He skillfully illustrates each with the life example of outstanding Christian preachers, evangelists or missionary statesmen who reflect a shining testimony of each of the keys discussed.

The author's methodology is simple but effective. In each chapter he first identifies the secret he is presenting. Next, he presents an excellent biblical/pastoral exposition about the secret. Lastly, he exemplifies the secret through the biography of an appropriate historical personality, thereby showing that the discipline the key refers to is achievable

The important keys discussed in this book include: Walking with God, Going on to Deeper Sanctification, Maintaining Holiness, Sustaining a Healthy Devotional Life, Humility and Brokenness, Transparency, Maintaining Productive Work Habits, Integrity, Accountability, Simplicity and Frugality, Life-Long Student, Family Focus and Growing Older with Grace.

These vital keys are exemplified not only in the lives of several biblical characters, but also in the lives of historical figures. It is hoped that with appropriate understanding and application of *Secrets of Ministerial Success*, the Nigerian Church would ignite our long-awaited revival and thereby fulfill her ministry and mandate.

This book has come in the fullness of time to arouse all Christians and lovers of religious freedom, to ignite the revival fire in Nigerian Churches, to instigate spiritual capacity building among Christians and to stem the rising tide of Islamization in Nigeria. The issues raised in this book are fundamental and germane to the survival of Christianity in Nigeria and therefore should be read not only by ministers but by every Christian, for spiritual empowerment and deepening of their Christian faith in God.

I know the author of this book very well. He is a prolific writer, a dynamic preacher and teacher of the word of God, a brilliant and celebrated church historian, a church builder and the founder of two theological colleges in Nigeria. He is an unrepentant apostle of revival who emphasizes holy living. His views in this book should be taken seriously, most particularly in view of his maturity and experience in Christian service and ministry. He deserves our appreciation for writing this book. I predict it is destined to be a "best seller" and classic.

Prof E. M. Uka
Prelate Emeritus, Presbyterian Church of Nigeria
Professor in Residence, West Africa Theological Seminary
Lagos, Nigeria
July 2020

Preface

More than fifty years ago Emma Lou and I knelt at the front of an auditorium in Milan, Illinois, USA, and were together ordained into the Christian ministry. On that day we became Rev. and Rev. Mrs. Gary S. Maxey. We were launched on a journey that was to take us outside of the USA for most of the next fifty-plus years. It was a journey that was to give us the opportunity to evangelize the lost, pastor the flock of God and train several thousand spiritual leaders.

We were following the footsteps of our parents. Emma Lou's parents were ordained ministers, and had co-pastored churches in Idaho, Colorado, Pennsylvania and Illinois. My father, too, was an ordained pastor, as was his own father. They were both also trainers of pastors. For eighteen years my father pastored churches in Idaho, Nebraska, Texas and Illinois. For thirty-five years he taught ministerial students and travelled nationally and internationally in all kinds of pastoral training settings.

Gleaning from my own experiences and those of my wife, from my in-laws and from my own side of our extended family, combined with my decades of living seriously every day with the Bible, I humbly believe there is much I can share about what it takes to succeed in Christian ministry. Increasingly over the past years I have had many come to me and ask me to mentor them. It is impossible for me to do so face-to-face and on a regular basis with all those who make that request. However, this book distills much of what I would share with any such eager searcher for sound mentoring.

As I read the available literature today, I am often surprised about the surprising percentage of pastors who stumble in their ministerial calling and eventually drop out. They start, but they do not end well. Obviously, not everyone finds the pastoral life an easy path to travel. That is why after all these years I am moved to share with my readers, and most especially with my students (both past and present), what I believe are some of the fundamental secrets I have discovered about success in the ministry.

I have spent most of my life in Africa. Nigeria has become my reasonably comfortable and certainly beloved earthly home, even though heaven is where I have maintained my permanent address. I love Africa. I have often wished I had been born here, especially when I meet a fellow missionary with that kind of blessing. I have also wished I physically looked more like my African brothers and sisters. But, alas, those are things I cannot change, and thinking in those directions is a waste of energy.

Much more importantly, I know I am committed to excellence in ministry. Anyone who has read my spiritual autobiography, Confessions of a Grateful Pilgrim, knows I have not always been worthy of emulation in my ministry. I have done more than my share of stumbling in life. I do not say that out of modesty, but more out of regret and often even shame. Thankfully, though, I have also learned how to get back up and move on. Life is too short to waste time crying about our missteps and to moan over missed opportunities and failed adventures, though God knows that I do just that from time to time.

For any success I may have had in my journey, I owe an incalculable debt to my amazing wife, Emma Lou. We were made for each other, though I definitely got the far better deal in the bargain. It is true that we both spent too many years of our married life before we dug down to uncover the roots of some of the great dysfunctions we brought to our marriage from our growing-up years. But the journey has been amazingly rewarding and has been crowned with God's abundant blessings in ways that are too many to count.

Over the past fifty-plus years Emma Lou and I have almost always engaged in a flurry of ministry activities. We still marvel that God can use flawed and stumbling people for his glory, and that we were most of the time excited about the journey we were taking. Yet even in the darkest hours I am deeply grateful that Emma Lou held tightly to Jesus. Today she is my super-hero. She is more beautiful than ever and achieving more for God than I could ever have imagined in earlier years. Twenty-five years ago, she was not sure she wanted to continue life, but today she can't get enough of it! Thanks, Emma Lou.

Dr. Gary S. Maxey
1 August 2020
Lagos

WALKING WITH GOD

In some ways it must seem strange to start a summary of secrets to ministerial success by talking about something as basic as making sure I am walking with God. However, the fact is that there are ordained clergymen all over the world who have never entered into a vital personal relationship with God. That is surely a blight of major proportions on the Church. Such people are a danger to themselves and to everyone else around them. That is why I must begin my advice to my students by reminding us that the most fundamental quality of a minister of the gospel is knowing Jesus Christ in a vital saving relationship. Knowing God personally and doing whatever is necessary to maintain that relationship has to be the absolutely NUMBER ONE secret of our ministerial success.

For many years I have preached a simple sermon based on Matthew 7:13-27 which I borrowed from one of my early mentors, Rev. Foy Bullock. It is entitled "Four Tests of the

Kingdom." I have preached that sermon in at least ten countries around the world. I can know I am a true child of God if I pass four tests: the entrance test, the fruit test, the obedience test and the wisdom test.

The entrance test is vv. 13-14, which talk about entering through the strait gate to the narrow way that leads to salvation. If I am a born-again child of God, I will have clear knowledge that at a crucial juncture in my life I left the paths of sinful disobedience and entered into God's way of salvation. If I don't have that kind of testimony, I have not passed the entrance test.

Yet I must also pass the fruit test, in vv. 15-20. The fruit test is the examination of what is growing on my life "tree" as a result of my new birth. If my new birth is genuine, the resulting life will be marked not by fleshly fruit, but the fruit of the Spirit. Paul describes both kinds of fruit in Galatians 5. The works of the flesh include adultery, fornication, uncleanness, lewdness, idolatry, sorcery, hatred, contentions, jealousies, outbursts of wrath, selfish ambitions, dissensions, heresies, envy, murders, drunkenness, and revelries (Gal. 5:19-21). No matter what other qualifications I may appear to have, if any of those fruits are hanging on my personal tree I am disqualified. Some of them are more obvious than others, such as adultery, murder and drunkenness. But what about the "uncleanness" of secret pornographic addiction, or occasional out-of-control anger, or secret jealousy? The presence of such fruit in my life is a dead giveaway of a walk with God in need of restoration.

On the other hand, the fruit of the Spirit is what predominates in the life of a true believer. These include love, joy, peace, longsuffering, kindness, goodness, faithfulness, gentleness, self-control (vv. 22-23). Inspecting our lives to see the kind of fruit we are producing is a great test of the genuineness of our Christian life.

The third test of the kingdom is obedience. Matthew 7:21-23 underscores the importance of doing the will of God, or obeying God. Disobedience to God trumps any claims to godliness on my part, no matter how impressive my resume may be. Every child of God is characterized by ongoing obedience to the voice of God.

The final test, in verses 24-27, is the wisdom test. Our entire life must be built on Jesus Christ. He is my focus. Being a believer has to do with my entire life, in all of its aspects. Christ must be the foundation on which everyone in my life stands. If so, I will never fall!

There are a lot of practical questions that follow from what I have said. Am I totally clear on the fact that I have handed my life entirely over to God? Are there signs of fleshly fruit in my life that give hints that I am not who I think or say I am? Is there any hidden and unconfessed sin of uncleanness or immorality that no one but I know about? Do I harbor selfish ambition or envy or bitterness that others may not easily see? On the other hand, can I honestly say that my life is ruled by things like love, long-suffering and gentleness? All of these are practical measures for me to gauge the depth of my Christian walk.

PERSONAL SPIRITUAL NURTURE

I want to say more about this later, but it is important to underscore the fact that if I am to maintain a healthy walk with God I must find great ways to nurture myself. The reason is that the life of Christ within me is like any living thing. It must be nurtured in order for it to thrive.

How do a new mother and father respond to the birth of their first child? Do they put the child in a corner and then go about their lives as though the child does not exist, or maybe just checking up on it every day or two? No way! They are homed in on the need for that child to be nourished and cared for, hour by hour. And so also it is with my own spiritual life. If I neglect it, I can expect it to weaken and eventually die. Yet if I am careful to nurture it, I can see it grow and thrive and mature.

Or suppose I decide to purchase a guard dog to provide protection for my family, and perhaps also some enjoyment for my children. I go out and find a new-born puppy and bring it home. As a family we do all we can to learn how to take proper care of our new possession. We ensure it is fed proper food and given proper care. We will not bring the puppy home and then neglect it and leave it to starve and die.

In like manner, when I welcome the life of the Holy Spirit into my own being, I must take pains to nurture that life within me. It is not something I do haphazardly. Just as a steady and predictable diet of food and water is of optimum benefit for my body, so a steady and predictable diet of spiritual nourishment is what will enable me to grow strong spiritually.

An uncompromising daily devotional routine is at the foundation of my personal spiritual nurture. That means that especially as a minister of the gospel I will read the Bible every day. For many years my personal habit has been to read the scriptures daily in three different translations, and from three different places in the Bible. On any given morning I am almost always reading two portions in the Old Testament and one in the New Testament, and usually each of them using a difference English translation. I do not read lengthy portions on most days (often not more than one chapter in each of the translations). I must continually take the word of God into my mind and heart with this kind of devotional reading.

To further nurture my walk with God I should at least on a weekly basis seek to memorize small portions of the Bible. Committing scripture to memory has benefits that cannot be obtained in any other way. Some people find memorization of scripture relatively easy, but most of us struggle to keep up this kind of discipline. However, do not be discouraged! Memorizing only one verse a week is a worthy accomplishment!

Having a time of daily personal prayer is the capstone of personal spiritual nurture. One of the most fundamental things I will carry out of this world is my relationship with God. Though there are still many mysteries about what lies beyond the grave, surely eternity must involve more intimate communication with God. My daily prayer time is literally practicing up for heaven! As I grow in my relationship with God, I learn to do what Paul calls prayer "without ceasing." That means the attitude of my heart is one of continually turning to God with praise, with calls for his presence, appeals for his wisdom, etc. Prayer is the breath of the believer.

Finally, it is healthy and strengthening to read supplemental literature that feeds my soul, on a daily basis. The reading of daily devotional books is a great idea. The devouring of excellent Christian biographies should be a steady part of my reading diet.[1] By engaging in that kind of reading I regularly bring into my personal orbit great men and women of past ages who have proven themselves as worthy models for Christian emulation. Making myself a friend of the great men and women who have gone before me will go far in strengthening my Christian life.

WISELY HANDLING FAILURE

Proverbs 4:18 has fascinated me for many years, and I especially like the way it is translated in the NIV: "The path of the righteous is like the morning sun, shining ever brighter till the full light of day." What that verse teaches us is that normal Christian life is a walk of progressive spiritual growth. It is a journey of progress, from the point when we are born again until we finally lay our armor down and enter the heavenly portals for all of eternity. Walking with God, if it is nourished by a steady diet of the word of God, prayer, and obedience to the voice of God

---

[1] See Gary S. Maxey, *Going Deeper with God* (Lagos: WATS Publications, 2020), 55-62.

means we gradually mature and become stronger through the seasons of life.

However, it would be a huge mistake to assume or teach that Christian life is without trials, temptations, and occasional backsets and even sometimes enormous stumbling. The Bible is filled with warnings about the possibility of failure. Paul wisely warned the Corinthians, "Therefore let him who thinks he stands take heed lest he fall" (1 Cor. 10:12). Thankfully, he immediately went on to say, "No temptation has overtaken you except such as is common to man; but God is faithful, who will not allow you to be tempted beyond what you are able, but with the temptation will also make the way of escape, that you may be able to bear it" (v. 13).

I know what it is to stumble and fall in my walk with God, even to the point of once again living in deceit and hypocrisy. It is something I am ashamed to admit, even now. Sadly, I know what it is to carry my Bible into the pulpit and try to preach while knowing that I myself was not right with God. I wish that had never happened to me.

I am sure I could have avoided a lot of problems if I had received early lessons on how to respond to failures in my Christian walk. The truth is that I do not know of many great Christian people who have not had several backsets during their Christian pilgrimage. As much as we would like to believe that the Christian life is one of never-ending success, occasional stumbling and failure is frequently the norm.

I do believe in the truth of Proverbs 4:18. Our Christian lives generally involve forward and upward movement. We sometimes refer to it as progressive sanctification. However, I also know that does not mean there are not occasional times in our journey in which we mess up, disappoint ourselves and others, momentarily fail ourselves and others by listening to Satan's temptations. In those cases, we are eventually forced to stop and make things right. Those things are not inevitable, and need not and should not happen, yet they all too often do happen.

Please do not misunderstand me. I am not making excuses for failure. If I get the idea in my head that failure is normal it weakens my resolve to stand firm in the midst of temptation. On the other hand, God's promises are strong. He has assured us that we need not stumble. Jude ended his short epistle with these words: "Now to Him who is <u>able to keep you from stumbling</u>, and to present you faultless before the presence of His glory with exceeding joy, to God our Savior, who alone is wise, Be glory and majesty, dominion and power, both now and forever. Amen" (Jude 24,25). That should encourage us.

Yes, God can keep me from stumbling, but what if, after all, I do stumble? What should I do in such a case? One of the really bad ideas I had in my head as a young believer was that if I ever stumbled and deliberately did something wrong or sinful, I would have to go all the way back to Square One and start my spiritual journey all over.

In short, in my church we did not know how to handle the issue of deliberate sin in the life of believers. I therefore thought if I deliberately disobeyed God it meant I had completely lost my salvation. Therefore, now I was no better than the guilty sinner I was before I first came to Jesus. It took me many painful years to discover that I was getting truly bad advice. The problem was that no one had taught me how to handle failure.

Let's face it: there are many ways in which we can fail in our walk with God. It is possible to fail God by suddenly giving in to temptation and deliberately committing sin. Maybe in a flash of temptation I tell a big, fat lie to a brother or sister (or even a little, skinny one, for that matter), perhaps in order to save face. Perhaps I pocket some money that I know is not really my own and end up using it for my own selfish purposes. Or maybe I jump the rails and momentarily and deliberately savor forbidden pornography or lustful thoughts about a beautiful or sexy woman who is not my wife.

I can also experience spiritual failure by gradually neglecting the scriptures and the place of prayer and becoming so busy that I lose a sense of God's presence in my life. This is no doubt why the writer to the Hebrews says, "we must give the more earnest heed to the things we have heard, lest we drift away" (Heb. 2:1). Yes, it's possible to just drift away.

No matter who we are, I believe we will from time to time face situations of this nature, either suddenly or gradually discovering that we have gone backwards when we should have been going forward. So how should we respond?

I can tell you that in my early Christian days I totally failed myself and God by not handling failure wisely. For one thing, I accepted Satan's lie that since I had actually done something which I knew was wrong I was therefore out of fellowship with God, and I had gone all the way back to Square One. I thought I was no better off than all the other sinners in the world, and like them I would need to repent and get right with God all over again.

In fact, to make matters worse Satan then convinced me that since I had indulged in forbidden sin once again I might just as well wallow in it and do it over and over again, since I was surely no longer God's child. Oh, what a lie he sold to me! It cost me heavily, and it took me a long time to get back safely to the arms of Jesus.

So, here is the key: remember the sound advice of John in his first epistle. He says there loudly and clearly that he writes to his children so that they will not sin (1 John 2:1). He reminds them more than once that as born-again children of God we are known not as sinners but as saints who walk in obedience to God. However, he also quickly says, "But if anyone does sin, we have an advocate with the Father—Jesus Christ, the Righteous One" (1 John 2:1b).

John's very sane advice is that when I discover I have failed God I should quickly and confidently fly back to the arms of Jesus and accept his forgiveness and his intervention as my advocate. I should do it without wasting a single moment of time. Hallelujah! That is the answer. "Lord, I know I have sinned against you, and I am sorry. I accept your forgiveness. Help me to be strong in you."

One of my own weaknesses as a believer was that I brought into my Christian life from my childhood a belief that God was stingy with his love for me. I therefore more-or-less subconsciously believed that he was ready at any moment to quickly disown me if I deviated from the Christian path. In other words, I did not have an adequate picture of God's overwhelming love toward me. Yes, he very deeply loved little old me! And he still loves me, 24/7! That's why when I mess up, he is ready to receive me and hold me in his arms.

C. T. Studd—A Model of Christian Devotion

Much of the inspiration for my own life of devotion to God has come from studying the lives of great saints of God from past generations. I have spent much of my life at the feet of heroic predecessors whose examples have spurred me on to greater heights and deeper depths. I have discovered few examples of Christian devotion and self-denial that surpass that of Charles Thomas (C. T.) Studd, one of my great missionary heroes.

There is very much about Studd's life that can stir one's heart to a closer walk with God. As a young man he was a renowned athlete heralded throughout the British Empire and especially in his native England, where he was the most famous cricketer of his generation. On top of that, his father left him an enormous financial fortune. Yet he renounced both fame and fortune to travel to inland China as one of Hudson Taylor's missionaries.

When Studd turned twenty-five years of age and finally received his fortune (while he was already on service in China) he immediately gave away 100% of it to missionary causes all around the world. He spent the rest of his life as a faith missionary. He served fifteen years in China, six years in India, and then lived out his final nineteen years in the heart of Africa, serving in the northeastern Congo forests where no other missionaries had gone before.

To make matters even more challenging, C. T. Studd spent his long years in the heart of Africa away from his beloved wife, who remained behind in vigorous labors raising support for C. T. and dozens of others who eventually joined in the work. The places of his labor in the Congo eventually experienced mighty revival fires, extending long beyond his own death, at age seventy. So, what was his secret of success?

"Bwana Mukubwa," as he was affectionately known during his final years, lived alone in a small circular hut, with walls of split bamboo tied together with string, a grass roof and a dried mud floor. He slept on a native bed made from strips of goat hide tied to a wooden frame. Nearby was a shelf with several well-worn Bibles. It was his bedroom, dining room and living room all in one.

Near the foot of the bed was an open log fire on the dried mud floor. C. T.'s "boy," who was a full-grown man and his only attendant, slept curled up on the floor in front of the fire and every morning like clockwork would stir awake about 2:30 or 3:00 am, beat together a few sticks in the fireplace to knock off the burnt ends, and then blow the sparks into a flame. Then on with the kettle, and soon a cup of tea would be made. By this time Bwana would be awaken. The tea is handed to him, and the boy would go back to sleep again.

Now a Bible is taken down from the shelf, and Bwana is alone with God. What passed between them in those silent hours was known a few hours later to all who had ears to hear. At the native meeting in the morning lasting seldom less than three hours when Bwana took it, at the prayers with the whites at night lasting from 7 to 9 or 10 pm, what he had seen and heard alone with God in the early morning was poured out from a heart ablaze for the salvation of men, and hopes which had been touched with a live coal. He never needed more preparation for his meetings than those early hours. He didn't prepare. He talked with God, and God talked with him, and made His word live in him. He saw Jesus. He saw men and women going in their millions to hell. And he always said that that is all the preparation a man needs for preaching the Gospel, if it be a dozen times the same day. "Don't go into the study to prepare a sermon," he once said. "That is all nonsense. Go into your study to go to God and get so fiery that your tongue is like a burning coal and you've got to speak."[2]

---

[2] Norman Grubb, C. T. Studd: *Cricketer and Pioneer* (Fort Washington, PA: CLC Publications, 1933), Kindle loc 2609-2636.

I may not agree 100% with C. T. Studd's advice for sermon preparation (more of that later), but what I do agree with is that here was a man who was fixated on God because his life had been transformed through the New Birth. He later took time to experience the powerful cleansing of the Holy Spirit in a deeper sanctification experience. As a result, he spoke powerful words because he was truly a man in touch with God. That can, and must, be true of all of us who aspire to be ministers of God.

GOING ON TO DEEPER SANCTIFICATION

It is crystal clear from the scriptures that God yearns to walk with his children in unclouded fellowship. Other religions are usually about people seeking for God; yet the Bible message is about God seeking for us. In the earliest pages of scripture, we see the Creator God seeking to walk with Adam and Eve *"in the cool of the day"* (Gen. 3:8). Centuries later, Jesus said, *"The Son of Man has come to seek and to save that which was lost"* (Luke 19:10). We can deduce from this that when we are walking in daily fellowship with God we are in tune with the will of our Father.

Yet it goes deeper than that. God's desire is that we continually cherish and reach out for holiness of heart and life. *"Pursue peace with all people, and holiness, without which no one will see the Lord"* (Heb. 12:14). Our Heavenly Father urges us to proactively pursue after holiness. Paul expressed this to the Corinthians in this manner: *"Therefore, having these promises, beloved, let us cleanse ourselves from all filthiness of the flesh and spirit, perfecting holiness in the fear of God"* (2 Cor. 7:1).

My observation is that there are very few Christian pastors or teachers who would say that holiness is not important. We all at least pay lip service to the importance of holiness. Yet it appears to me that precious few can tell us with satisfying clarity just *how* we are to do that. Too many of us end up frustrated as a result.

The pursuit for holiness in our lives begins with our New Birth, but it does not end there. As new-born children of God, we have experienced the cleansing of regeneration. We instinctively feel that while we were unclean before we are now clean. That is why as new believers we are rightfully called not just children of God but *saints*. Sometimes we use that word loosely, but the Bible takes it seriously. The word *saint* means literally *holy one*. A saint has been made holy, through the blood of Jesus. *"Therefore Jesus also, that He might sanctify the people with His own blood, suffered outside the gate"* (Heb. 13:12).

What does that mean in practical terms? As saints of God, we walk in fellowship with our Master, in a life of daily obedience. We are admittedly full of faults and shortcomings and mistakes and occasional stumbles, yet we are walking in victory over sin, the flesh and the devil. Our names are written down in heaven. We are heirs and joint heirs with Christ. Even though we are imperfect, we are victorious.

However, if we continue to walk faithfully in obedience to God sooner or later we discover we are carrying around baggage within us that is not in clear harmony with God. If we are attentive to the voice of the Holy Spirit, sooner or later we begin to discover saboteurs within us that fight against our upward progress. It may take us a good while to see these things, and often our slowness in hearing clearly the voice of God is because we instinctively make excuses for our self. That explains why the spirit of pride, of carnal anger, or of self-centeredness is often more obvious to those around us than it is to ourselves.

However, if we continue to walk in obedience to God, sooner or later the Holy Spirit is faithful to show us inner characteristics, attitudes or inclinations that are inconsistent with the pure character of Christ. When that begins to happen, there is no reason to panic or despair, but only to realize that God wants to rid us of those things that are contrary to Christ within us. It is all a part of the journey of what could be labeled progressive sanctification.[3]

It is highly regrettable that theological prejudices sometimes enter in at this point. In some circles strong dogmatic objections have been raised against any idea of a distinct work of God's grace beyond our new birth experience, or what some have called a "second blessing."

---

[3]For more about this journey toward deeper holiness see Gary S. Maxey, *The Highway of Holiness* (Lagos: WATS Publications, 2018), and Gary S. Maxey, *The Thessalonian Road: Sanctification Made Plain* (Lagos: WATS Publications, 2019). I give my personal testimony about this journey in Gary S. Maxey, *Confessions of a Grateful Pilgrim: Reflections @ 70* (Lagos: WATS Publications, 2018), Chapter Four, "Discovering Holiness."

Perhaps some of the objections are in response to people who have been harsh and legalistic in their pronouncements. It is never helpful to try to pressure others into following a cookie-cutter religion where we blindly heed the dictates of man rather than the voice of the Holy Spirit.

I am talking about our need to listen to the quiet and convicting voice of the Spirit, as I discover things that require a deeper cleansing. Surely deep jealousy can reside even in the heart of a true child of God, yet that jealousy is not pleasing to God and should and can be conquered through a deeper cleansing. Volatile or even beneath-the-surface self-centered anger can also be a defeating reality in the life even of an otherwise on-fire saint of God. Yet it is inconsistent with the Spirit of Christ and ought not to be there. What I am talking about here is not taking sides in a theological argument, but simply listening to the gentle voice of God.

The Apostle Paul has a lot to say about this onward journey in the life of believers, leading them toward a deeper consecration and a deeper cleansing that will take them to a whole new level of purity and power. Not only in the New Testament but also down through the pages of Church history, there are innumerable testimonies about how God's people were led by the Holy Spirit into this triumph of deeper sanctification.[4] For some it has come fairly soon after their initiation into the heavenly kingdom, and for others it has come after many years of walking with the Savior.

One of the key questions at this point is the balance between a focus on power or a focus on purity. What is the primary reason for our need for a deeper sanctification? Is it that we should have more power for service or that we need a greater purity? The proper answer is that they are *both* important, but it is extremely important that we see how those two issues relate. The reason is that one of them is more fundamental or more foundational that the other. Perhaps I can explain it best by quoting from Commissioner Samuel Brengle, of the Salvation Army. In his book, *When the Holy Ghost is Come*, he writes:

> Many have looked at the promise of power when the Holy Ghost is come . . . and they have hastily and erroneously jumped to the conclusion that the baptism with the Holy Ghost is for work and service only. It does bring power—the power of God—and it does fit for service . . . the proclamation of salvation and the conditions of peace to a lost world; but not that alone, nor primarily. The primary, the basal work

---

[4] I deliberately use the term "deeper sanctification" because I want to avoid other terms that have become shibboleths for too many people, such as "baptism with the Holy Spirit," "entire sanctification," "the second blessing," etc. Pursuing holiness is not a matter of theological labeling. I am sure we will not be given a theology entrance examination when we pass through the valley of death and into eternity. "Deeper sanctification" here means God wants to take me to a new level of victorious Christian living by cleaning up things in my life that are contrary to Christ and giving me a new power to do his will and be better equipped for ministry.

of the baptism is that of cleansing. . . . The great hindrance in the hearts of God's children to the power of the Holy Ghost is inbred sin—that dark, defiant, evil something within that struggles for the mastery of the soul . . . and when the Holy Spirit comes, His first work is to sweep away that something, that carnal principle, and make free and clean all the channels of the soul. . . . This purification from sin is promised. . . . it is necessary. . . . [and this] deliverance is possible. . . . It is primarily for this that the Holy Ghost comes as a baptism of fire: that sin might be consumed out of us. . . ."[5]

No matter what the time factor, the first step in moving toward this deeper sanctification is a growing conviction of inner need. There is no way I can expect to experience the deeper cleansing God wants to bring about in my life unless and until I have a keen awareness of my inner uncleanness. It is not uncommon to walk with God in spiritual victory for many months or even years without a clear picture of this deeper inner need. However, we can be sure that our fleshly human pride, self-centered anger, secret jealousy and careless lustful thinking are an afront to God. These are things that pollute us from the inside out. If we never see it, we will obviously not seek for its remedy.

When I find myself gripped with anger against others because they have offended my ego, or when they have disregarded my authority, or otherwise stepped on my toes,

---

[5]Samuel Logan Brengle, *When the Holy Ghost is Come* [originally published in 1909] (Atlanta: The Salvation Army, 1982), 31-36.

I can be sure there is a unChristlike spirit within me that needs to be crucified. I may keep myself under firm control and not allow the anger to embarrass me before others, yet it is definitely not the spirit of Christ.

Secret envy is a problem for many believers. The heart that has not experienced deeper sanctification secretly (and sometimes not so secretly) yearns for ego-pleasing recognition. There may be a fine line between what is acceptable to God and what needs to receive a death blow. It is only the Holy Spirit who can reveal the need of our heart.

When others are preferred over us, we may find it impossible to truly rejoice with them. We may find ourselves secretly wishing ill of them, in the hidden recesses of our heart. The reason is that there is a unChristlike spirit of jealousy brewing within us. It is part of the Adamic nature we have inherited from our original parents, and that needs to be taken to the cross of Christ and thoroughly crucified.

One of the most helpful things we can do in these situations is to sit under anointed preachers who understand the workings of the fleshly mind and who are used of God to expose our hearts to the undiluted gaze of the Holy Spirit. David cried out, *"Search me, O God!"* (Ps. 139:23). That should also be our own cry. That made a huge difference for me as a young believer. Some of the preachers I listened to were not highly educated. They did not always have their theology as straight as the Apostle Paul. But they knew how to preach down conviction on those who were unwittingly nursing unclean hearts. Such people are invaluable in kingdom work.

Another helpful exercise is to read the biographies of great saints of past ages who have also traveled this path. It is amazing that in hundreds of different cultures and different ages God's pathway to greatness has always taken his people through the valley of crucifixion of the fleshly nature. That is why we must force ourselves to STOP long enough to allow the illumination of the Holy Spirit to flood our hearts until everything that is unlike Jesus is exposed.

It is also an exciting thing that once God has taken us through that valley of personal crucifixion and exposed our need to the point where we cry out for deliverance, he will then turn around and demand a consecration from us we have never before thought possible. These are private and personal issues, yet every child of God needs to experience that harrowing journey where God demands us to slay our Isaac, to give up our fondest dreams, to accept the seemingly unacceptable, in our drive to be all he wants us to be.

Oh, the sweet agony of total surrender to God! God must take us a million miles away from the glaring lights of the cathedral and the tawdry barking of the crowd manipulators. We must stand naked in his presence long enough to see ourselves as he sees us. When that happens, he can direct us to the deeper cleansing that is the birthright of every child of God. Happy is the man or the woman who knows what this is about. They are the ones most fit to excel for Jesus and for his Church.

My appeal is for us to have a light hold on theological labels at this point. Gaining keen theological insights is a lifelong pursuit, and always more or less flawed. Even when we get to heaven that journey will have just begun. I have often said that I believe I will spend the first part of my life in eternity laughing at myself and how dim my earthly understanding really was. Paul says we see *"through a mirror, dimly"* (1 Cor. 13:12). Remember that mirrors in Paul's day were not nearly as good as in our day!

My delight is to fully abandon myself to the gentle voice and persuasion of the Holy Spirit, whose great work is to convince all of us of *"sin, and of righteousness, and of judgement"* (John 16:8). If we do that with an open heart, I am persuaded we will all be led into what I have been talking about. Hallelujah!

The Secret of D. L. Moody's Power

Hardly was any man less likely to become the 19th century's most successful soul-winner and evangelist than Dwight L. Moody. He eventually evangelized at least one hundred million people and saw one million come to Christ. He never finished primary school and for much of his life could not write or speak proper English. Yet from the time he was born again at age eighteen he nurtured a passion to lead others to Christ. Even when he was rejected by others for his uncouth ways, he continued to teach and preach as best he could, while others were embarrassed and urged him to keep silent.

By dint of determination, energy and zeal, Moody eventually rose to the attention of others and found himself preaching to hundreds and then to thousands. In 1870 he teamed up with a singer and musician, Ira D. Sankey. Together they toured the USA and the United Kingdom. While in Ireland, Moody overhead words that changed his life: "The world has yet to see what God will do with and for and through a man who is fully and wholly committed to Him." Moody said to himself, "I'll be that man."

An even greater change came in 1871. Moody had been working hard, but according to his successor, R. A Torrey, "He had no real power. He worked largely in the energy of the flesh." That is when God began to use two faithful women who led Moody into the Spirit-filled life for which he longed.

Sara Anne Cooke and her widowed friend, Mrs. Hawxhurst, sat on the front row of Moody's church every service. While he preached, they prayed, as he could clearly see. At the close of each service, they would come up and greet him and thank him, saying, "We're praying for you." This finally exasperated Moody, and he said, "Why don't you pray for the unsaved?" They quietly answered, "We are praying that you may get the power."

This perplexed Moody. He had about the largest church in Chicago by that time, and the work seemed to be booming. Surely God was blessing him. But the ladies prayed on.

After two months an overpowering spiritual hunger affected his soul. He went to them and said, "I wish you would tell me what you mean." They testified to him and prayed with him that he would experience a deeper cleansing and be filled with the fulness of the Holy Spirit.

Moody testified, "There came a great hunger into my soul. I did not know what it was. I began to cry as I never had before. The hunger increased. I really felt that I did not want to live any longer if I could not have this power for service."

The women kept praying. One Friday as they prayed together, Moody prayed, "Lord baptize me with the Holy Spirit and fire." Days later, as he found himself in New York City, walking down Wall Street praying, suddenly God answered his prayer, and the power of the Holy Spirit fell on him. Moody rushed to the house of a friend where he could be alone. He stayed there alone in a room for hours, with God. The Holy Spirit flooded his soul with power and joy again and again until at last he asked God to hold it back or he would die on the spot from joy. Moody left that room with the power of God upon him and filling him.

What was the result? Moody said, "I went to preaching again. The sermons were not different; I did not present any new truths; and yet hundreds were converted." He added, "May God forgive me if I should seem to speak in a boastful way, but I do not know that I have preached a sermon since but God has given me some soul. I would not be back where I was before that experience for all the wealth of the world."[6]

After Moody's death, his good friend and fellow minister, J. Wilbur Chapman, who was himself widely known for his holy Christian character, said this in the Preface of his Moody biography,

> I write because I loved him, and I felt that I might in this way pay tribute to the most consistent Christian man I have ever known. I am confident that there has not been in these latter days a man who was more truly filled with the Holy Ghost than he. . . . I question if this generation has known a man who was more Christlike than D. L. Moody.[7]

The fiery cleansing of the Holy Spirit is what made all of the difference for a Dwight Moody, and it will also make all of the difference for all of the rest of us. By opening himself up to the promptings of the Holy Spirit Moody was able to receive a new lease on a life of deeper sanctification than he had ever known before. That same secret is available to all of us.

---

[6]Wesley L. Duewel, *Heroes of the Holy Life: Biographies of Fully Devoted Followers of Christ* (Grand Rapids: Zondervan, 2002), loc 1794-1900.
[7]J. Wilbur Chapman, *The Life and Work of D. L Moody* (Philadelphia: Universal Publishing Co., 1900), *25 Classic Christian Biographies* (Classic Christian Ebooks), Kindle loc 9808.

MAINTAINING HOLINESS

In his second epistle to the Corinthians Paul gave a double-barreled admonition: *"Therefore, having these promises, beloved, let us cleanse ourselves from all filthiness of the flesh and spirit, perfecting holiness in the fear of God"* (2 Cor. 7:1). His first concern and admonition had to do with their need for pure hearts. They needed to be cleansed from *"all filthiness of the flesh and spirit."* That is exactly what the Holy Spirit does for all believers who pursue after the deeper sanctification I talked about in the last chapter.

If we continue on as believers without ever seeing and seeking deliverance from those things in our fleshly nature that militate against godliness, we will most likely sooner or later cool off and perhaps even fall away. That is precisely why the writer to the Hebrews cried out (as I can imagine, with a loud voice): *"Therefore, since a promise remains of entering His rest, let us fear lest any of you seem to have come short of it"* (Heb. 4:1). The "rest" to which he was referring was the rest of a fully sanctified and Spirit-filled life. It is a fearful thing for us to go half-way with the Lord in our spiritual journey and then fall short of the deeper cleansing we so urgently need.

There is a second concern Paul expresses in 2 Corinthians 7:1 – not just that the Corinthians should be cleansed from all *"filthiness of the flesh and spirit,"* but that they would *"perfect holiness in the fear of God."* That second part of his double-barreled appeal refers to our need to *maintain* the holiness without which no one will see the Lord. That is what I want to talk about in this chapter: how do I ensure that I not only am sanctified through and through, but that I do all that is necessary to continue on in the life of holiness?

One of the great yet simple secrets toward this goal is what Paul expressed to his beloved disciples in Colossae. He told them, *"As you therefore have received Christ Jesus the Lord, so walk in Him, rooted and built up in Him and established in the faith, as you have been taught, abounding in it with thanksgiving"* (Col. 2:6-7). What he is saying is that whatever it took for you to receive Christ Jesus as your Lord you should maintain and continue in. That is the thing that will enable you to be rooted and built up in him.

I can easily illustrate this from my own life. I was seventeen years and four months old when I received mighty Holy Ghost conviction for my sins. It was in the midst of a great camp meeting filled with fiery preaching and deep repentance all around. I literally trembled under conviction. My knees buckled and I went forward to an altar of prayer. It was the glorious beginning of a spiritual journey.

However, especially since I was a preacher's kid with too much accumulated and unheeded theology and formal religion in my head, I did not find Jesus that first night. Instead, I became a daily seeker after God. I was making confessions all around and restituting stolen money and property. I began laying aside everything questionable in my life. Every day I was on my knees calling out to God. I was not yet born again, but I was reading the Bible every day. I attended church every time the doors were open. Whenever they would open the altar for prayers for lost sinners, I was the first one to rush forward. I was dead in earnest to get right with God and forever leave my life of sin and disobedience. I stopped lying, stealing and cheating. I was determined to obey God.

I do not blame God at all that it took me three solid months of such serious seeking for God until I broke through to a joyous witness of the Holy Spirit that I was born again. When it finally happened, I was filled with so much joy that it seemed my body would burst asunder.

My point here is that as soon as I was born again, I realized, just as Paul told the Corinthians, that just as I had received Christ Jesus the Lord, so now in the same manner I must walk in him. In other words, what got me into favor with God was what would keep me there. My spiritual life was like a great fire that had been kindled, and the only way I could be sure to maintain my relationship with God would be to keep rekindling that fire. I knew that fire would be rekindled through the same kind of daily praying, reading of the scriptures, listening to the voice of God, and obeying his guidance.

Interestingly, precisely the same issues were at stake months later when God showed me my need for a pure heart. After walking with God for at least four months in the unbroken bliss of salvation I began to discover a troubling doublemindedness in my life. At first, I would not allow myself to acknowledge the truth about it, but eventually I could not explain away the fact that there were unChristlike tendencies deep within me that were warring against me as a believer. No one but I knew about that battle going on within. To all outward appearances I was still a shining example of Christian living.

However, there was eventually just too much fleshliness for me to deny. It included fleshly anger, jealousy, and especially an exceedingly ugly inner pride. I finally had no choice but to throw up my hands and declare openly that I needed a deeper cleansing. Thankfully, there were mature believers around me who knew exactly what I was facing, and who urged me to not spare myself in seeking God for a pure heart.

Once again, I found myself on a daily basis with a singular focus: "God, I must be rid of these saboteurs in my heart. I must be cleansed. Rid me of these things that fight against myself and against you!" It was a commitment to prayer, confession, and consecration that now consumed my attention day and night. And finally, after 87 days of passion-filled seeking, the fire of God once again fell, this time burning up the dross of inbred sin and purifying my soul to the depths. Hallelujah!

It is important to remember that we are neither saved, nor taken into deeper sanctification, by virtue of our own works. The Bible makes that amply clear. Yet we can never expect to reach heaven if after experiencing these important crisis experiences in our lives we neglect to walk in daily obedience to God as his dear children. As my long-time friend, John Oswalt, loves to say: "The way to God is by grace; the walk with God is by obedience."

SPIRITUAL MAINTENANCE PRIORITIES

There are a multitude of responsibilities we must shoulder if we are to maintain a consistent and growing walk with God. The truth is that there is no state of grace from which we cannot fall away this side of the grave, if we grow careless and negligent or if we give in to the strong temptations of Satan. What are the areas which should be of greatest concern to us?

<u>Continuing Consecration</u> should be of primary concern to us. It is impossible to be born again without surrendering our lives to God in consecration. Yet later on, as we continue to walk with God, in order for us to experience deeper sanctification God always first takes us through a much deeper consecration process which is always tailor-made for our own personality and life. That consecration usually involves surrender of our personal will in the areas of money and material possessions, the release of our closest human ties into the hands of God in a manner we have never before known and placing ourselves on God's altar as never before.

However, consecration is never a one-time issue. It has to be maintained. It also means we must take care that we do not knowingly or unknowingly take off of God's altar things we have previously surrendered. We can also be sure that as we reach crucial junctures in our life God will once again ask us to give up cherished dreams, or to slay our Isaacs on his altar. Continuing consecration is important.

<u>Steadfast Faith</u> in God is of daily importance in maintaining the holy life. The Bible is blunt in telling us that *"without faith it is impossible to please God"* (Heb. 11:6). We come to God as unbelievers *by faith*. We receive forgiveness of our sins *by faith*. We seek God for deeper cleansing *by faith*. And we receive the blessing of cleansing and the fulness of the Holy Spirit *by faith*. Why, therefore, would we not see that our daily walk with God as holy men and women is also *by faith?*

There are many days in my life in which I go to the word of God and the place of prayer and I feel completely empty of human emotion. If I were to measure my salvation by my feelings, I could quickly rank myself as an unbeliever. But I refuse to do that. Why? Because I am living by faith. I know that *"The Lord is not slack concerning His promise, as some count slackness, but is longsuffering toward us"* (2 Pet. 3:9). I can repeat back to God his own promise in Isaiah 26:3, *"You will keep him in perfect peace, Whose mind is stayed on You, because he trusts in You."* That is how I can and must maintain constant faith in the Lord.

Some people (including myself in former years) have stumbled over the fact that our spiritual emotions are not always as high as they may have been during the earliest months and years of our spiritual journey. That is often a signal to Satan to come and whisper in our ears that perhaps we have lost out spiritually and no longer have that same joy in the Lord we once had and therefore perhaps we are even backslidden. Beware! That sounds suspiciously like the voice of Satan. It is the signal for us to deliberately renew our commitment to steadfast faith in God.

<u>Habitual Communion</u> with God is fundamental to the maintaining of a holy life. Imagine for a moment what a marriage would look like if a husband and wife with full capabilities to converse together on a regular basis were to stop talking to each other and go through day after day without communication. In such a case one could only assume that something is dreadfully wrong, and in need of immediate correction. The same is true with our relationship with God. If Satan can manage to get us into a slump of silence between ourselves and God, he has certainly at least temporarily outsmarted us. Yet the remedy is at hand and within our own power. Why not suspend what you are doing right now and talk to God? He is listening.

<u>Consistent Bible Study</u> is another important factor in maintaining a life of holy living. It is not possible to make a valid claim as a minister of the gospel without a serious commitment to the study of scripture. By continuing to dig into the word of God on a daily and disciplined basis we can be sure to hear from God exactly what we need to remain strong and vigilant spiritually.

<u>A Clear Testimony to the Grace of Sanctification</u> has long been advocated by holiness proponents as important to the maintaining of that experience. The psalmist declares, *"Let the redeemed of the LORD say so"* (Ps. 107:2). When I was a child, we used to sing in Sunday school, "If you're saved and you know it, say 'AMEN!'" Then we would all shout "AMEN!" I am sure some of us did not know what we were singing, but there was truth in that Sunday school chorus. If we have experienced the grace of deeper sanctification and know in a practical sense what it is to be filled with all the fulness of the Holy Spirit, it is good to give a clear testimony to that effect. It is said that John Fletcher, whom John Wesley declared to be the holiest man he had ever known, lost the experience of deeper sanctification five times because of his hesitancy to affirm it.

The cultivation of a <u>Self-Denying Spirit</u> is yet another means of maintaining the holy life. There is within the heart of every fully sanctified man or woman a strong inclination to deny self and do whatever is necessary to exalt Jesus and in honor prefer others. We do not cling to our privileges as though they are guaranteed or our inalienable rights. The description of the *kenosis* of Jesus given by Paul in Philippians 2:5 11 should never be far from our consideration. Jesus let go of every possible divine prerogative in order to stand in our own stead, especially as he hung on the cross.

<u>Growth in Grace</u> is the characteristic of every born-again child of God, and it is doubly characteristic of those who have fully consecrated themselves to God and experienced

the deeper cleansing of the Holy Spirit. The impediments that hindered us prior to that deeper cleansing were many, including divided loyalties, selfish ambition, seeking of position and recognition, petty jealously, fleshly anger, nagging lustfulness, etc. With the conquering of those inner foes, there is every reason now for us to grow in grace on a daily basis.

Ultimately, it is the blossoming forth of the fruit of the Spirit that becomes more evident than ever in the life of a believer filled with the fulness of the Holy Spirit. Love, joy, peace, and all the other fruits of the Spirit are more evident than ever. At the same time, there are still human foibles, misjudgments, undiscovered prejudices, faulty memory, etc., that remind us that we are not yet in our glorified bodies.

Francis Asbury: Apostle of Holy Living

During the first generation of America's history as a nation there was a long list of people who became national heroes: George Washington, Benjamin Franklin, John Adams, Thomas Jefferson, and many others. Everyone in America knew who these men were. Their fame eventually spread around the world. However, there is one man who saw more Americans face-to-face during their generation than any of them. This man, whose face was more recognized, respected and revered than them all, was the ubiquitous Father of American Methodism, Francis Asbury.

Asbury arrived in the American colonies in 1771, sent by John Wesley to care for Methodists who had already crossed the Atlantic from England. Over the next 45 years Asbury traveled an average of 6,000 miles every year, through the roughest imaginable weather and terrain, crossing the rugged and at time almost trackless Allegheny mountains 60 times.

The secret to Asbury's success certainly included the fact that he was a sanctified man. After his conversion, we went on to experience a further and deeper cleansing and infilling with the fulness of the Holy Spirit. It was doubtlessly because of that experience that he eventually offered himself to go to America. He was the second son of his parents but had lost his older sibling during childhood. Yet despite his great love for his parents he was willing to sail to America and never see them again.

Asbury, though eventually greatly loved by thousands of both Methodists and non-Methodists in his adopted land, shunned undue publicity and could not be persuaded to allow a portrait to be made of himself until he had been in America for 23 years, and ten years after he was made a bishop. What sustained Asbury through four-plus decades of service in America was the steadfastness of his Christian commitment and discipline.

Because he was incessantly on the road making the rounds to many hundreds of preaching points, Asbury deliberately never married. Despite his rigorous travels he unfailingly rose every morning at 5:00 am, spending one hour in prayer each morning, and one hour in the evening. He wrote in his journal, "Oh, how I wish to spend all my time and talents for Him who spilt His blood for me."

One of the typical prayers he would say, even on his way to America, was "Lord, we are in thy hands and in thy work. Thou knowest what is best of us and for thy work; whether plenty or poverty. The hearts of all men are in thy hands. If it is best for us and for thy church that we should be cramped and straitened, let the people's hands and hearts be closed: If it is better for us; for the church,—and more to thy glory that we should abound in the comforts of life; do thou dispose the hearts of those we serve to give accordingly: and may we learn to be content whether we abound, or suffer need."[8]

Francis Asbury had an especially tender heart for the oppressed African American slaves. He reached out to them at every opportunity and welcomed them into the Methodist fold. At one point he met with President George Washington and made a strong appeal to him to free his own slaves, which Washington eventually did as a part of his last will and testament. On June 23, 1776 Asbury wrote in his journal, "After preaching at the Point, I met the class, and then met the black people, some of whose unhappy masters forbid their coming for religious instruction. How

---

[8]Duren, William Larkin. 1928. *Francis Asbury, Founder of American Methodism and Unofficial Minister of State, New York*: The Macmillan Company, 119-120.

will the sons of oppression answer for their conduct, when the great Proprietor of all shall call them to an account!"[9]

At another point Asbury wrote in his journal, "Bless the Lord, O ye saints! Holiness is the element of my soul. My earnest prayer is that nothing contrary to holiness may live in me." He was a remarkable man whose life example demonstrates for all of us the need to not only be filled with the fulness of the Holy Spirit but to live disciplined lives that will ensure the maintaining of that wonderful blessing.[10]

---

[9]Matthew Friedeman, *Swallowed Up in God, The Best of Francis Asbury's Journal and Letters* (Jackson, MS: Teleos Press, 2014).
[10]Wesley L. Duewel, *Heroes of the Holy Life: Biographies of Fully Devoted Followers of Christ* (Grand Rapids: Zondervan, 2002), Kindle, loc 93-234.

SUSTAINING A HEALTHY DEVOTIONAL LIFE

Closely related to both of the issues I have already mentioned is the discipline of a daily devotional life. I have discovered that when we are allowed to peek deeply enough into the lives of men and women of great achievement for God, we always discover that they prioritized finding time to nurture their relationship with God through a disciplined devotional life.

Once again, Bishop Francis Asbury comes to mind as a prime example. As I noted in the last chapter, he was the Father of American Methodism. He travelled to the American colonies at twenty-six years of age as John Wesley's emissary to the fledgling Methodists, in the days leading up to the American Revolution. He never went back to England and never married. He lived on as an indefatigable horse-back superintendent for forty-five years. It was an incredibly tough 70-year life, and Asbury did it without complaint even though he was physically ill much of the time. Occasionally he had to be literally tied onto the back of his horse so he could make it to his next appointment.

In Darius Salter's biography of Asbury, he shares this telling excerpt from Asbury's journal:

> This morning I ended the reading of my Bible through in about four months. It is hard work for me to find time for this; but all I read and write I owe to early rising. If I were not to rise always by five, and sometimes at four o'clock, I should have no time only to eat my breakfast, pray in the family, and get ready for my journey – as I must travel every day.[11]

I can assure us that Asbury's statement, "it is hard work for me to find time for this," has been the testimony of multitudes of other great men and women of God. Asbury was into the word of God in the pre-dawn hours every day during the days before electricity. Reading through the Bible in about four months would mean reading an average of ten chapters daily. I am not saying that this is the inevitable standard for each of us, but at least we can understand why people like Asbury were walking concordances of the scriptures and why they had power when they went into the pulpit.

I love the way Eugene Peterson paraphrases 1 Tim. 4:7-8 in *The Message – "Exercise daily in God – no spiritual flabbiness, please! Workouts in the gymnasium are useful, but a discipline life*

---

[11]Darius Salter, *America's Bishop: The Life of Francis Asbury* (Nappanee, IN: Francis Asbury Press, 2003), 73.

in God is far more so, making you fit both today and forever." We live in a day of progressively greater consciousness and advocacy for physical fitness.

My father lived a relatively sedentary life during the latter decades of his adult life and managed to keep going until age 82. Yet things are different today. Nowadays I am bombarded with admonitions that I must not neglect "workouts in the gymnasium," in one form or the other. So, unless I am feeling ill, I dutifully get on my treadmill at least three times a week until I am sweaty, exhausted and ready to drop (and I can even hear some readers thinking, "That's not enough!").

Yet according to Eugene Peterson, Paul says, *"exercise <u>daily</u> in God . . . making you fit both today and forever."* Here is the bottom line: all around us there is a constant hue and cry for more power and for a more effective fulness of the Holy Spirit. Yet strangely, many of us continue to be careless and neglectful of the most fundamental God-appointed means by which power and effectiveness for God are achieved. It is like the spectator who sees an awe-inspiring musical or athletic performance and blurts out, "I would love to be able to do that!"

Years ago, before I was born again, I aspired to become a great concert pianist. I worked night and day for five years, starting at twelve years of age, trying to achieve it. I went through many long months in which I was at the piano keyboard often more than ten hours daily, nearly driving my family crazy in the process. However, I eventually discovered that there were not enough hours in the day to turn me into a world-class musician.

I finally abandoned it, though that decision was primarily due to the fact that at age seventeen I found Jesus. I realized that music and my dream of fame and fortune thereby had become my egotistical idol. I must admit, however, that even today, when I listen to the majesty of a Beethoven or Grieg piano concerto, I sometimes foolishly fantasize about being the person on the piano bench. But all to no avail. Why? I have not paid the price.

For my spiritual life, however, there is a fundamental difference. Being a godly man or woman does not require supernormal talent. No matter who I am, I can and I will pay the price, because spiritual excellence is possible for *all of us*. Unlike the rare mastery of the top musical or athletic performances, there is no one among us who cannot excel in our devotion to God. The reason many do not succeed is that they are consuming up to twelve hours daily to take care of their bodies—eating, drinking, bathing, clothing, sleeping, etc.—but are squeezing out only minutes for the care of their souls.

Let me be practical. I have listened to some Christian leaders who have foolishly paraded quite unrealistic standards before their followers. I remember a well-known Nigerian evangelist who told his audience that any Christian who was not spending at least three hours daily in prayer was not qualified to call himself Christian. Just recently I heard a very good friend of mine who is also a respected leader telling his followers that they should be praying in tongues "several hours a day."

My personal opinion is that advice like that is not only not helpful but is positively harmful. I view it as similar to telling an aspiring high-jump athlete that he should begin by jumping over his house every day. The reality is that even if he tries, he will likely break his leg or crack his head open.

Having said all of that, however, let me most candidly and seriously say that anyone who has been called into ministry and who is engaging in the work of God as a pastor, evangelist, counselor or superintendent should be giving at least one solid hour every day to the nurturing of his or her own soul. Hopefully there are many who have expanded beyond that one hour. I am talking about focused, loving, uninterrupted devotion with the Lord Jesus over an open Bible. We must daily receive refreshment from God. Our spiritual lives must be refueled.

When we do this kind of thing on a consistent daily basis, we can expect God himself to teach us, strengthen us, and correct us. He will reveal his secrets to us, and it is through this kind of process that spiritual giants are gradually formed. To the contrary, when we neglect these exercises, we remain spiritual weaklings, no matter how much fantasizing we do about being strong and victorious.

We can be sure that Satan will do everything in his power to keep us from our regular trysting place with God. He will get us to be irregular about it, and not even sure of when and where our trysts with God will take place. He will bring in a multitude of distractions and will convince us that we must hasten off to work before we have had time to hear clearly from God in adequate solitude.

The habits of my own daily private time with the Lord have been fixed for many years. From the moment I surrendered my life to Jesus at age seventeen my daily private time with the Lord was placed at the top of my priorities. Despite times of testing, trial and backsets I have never ceased to value this part of my life. I do not in any way pretend to be the sterling paradigm that others should mimic. But there have always been at least three elements in what I have done: systematic and meditative reading of scripture, reading of devotional and biographical excerpts from great saints of God, and prayer. Let me say something about each one.

Reading the scripture not so much as a scholar but as a suppliant before God is my first approach to daily devotional discipline. I want to hear from God through his holy word. Some people have told me that I need to hear from God through my dreams, or by listening to self-proclaimed prophets around me. Yet I remain convinced that overwhelmingly the most common means for God to speak to me is through his revealed word, the Bible.

I thirst to know more about the scriptures. I want them to guide me. So, every day I read the scriptures. Over the years I have read the scriptures in all of the languages with which I have at least a reasonable reading capacity—English, Spanish, French, and German. I have read much of the

New Testament in its original Greek. But what I do with regularity is to read the scriptures every day in three different English translations, which I alter every one or two years. All I am seeking to do is to hear from God and to engrave his word more deeply on my heart.

Reading from strong Christian devotional writers has also always been important to me, as well as the reading of Christian biographies. I usually do not read more than two to four pages at a sitting, but always enough to stir my heart to hear from God through the voices of people who usually have long since gone to their heavenly reward. [12]

The heart of my devotional time is prayer. Having attuned my heart to listen to God by digging into the scriptures and by hearing from great saints of by-gone days, I am now fully prepared to open my heart to God in praise, in heart-felt confession, in thanksgiving and in petition. Over the years I have frequently used a prayer list when it comes to the area of petition, as I pray for those whom God has laid on my heart. This includes family first and foremost, but beyond that to multitudes of others as I have been directed by God.

The most universally practiced guide to prayer is the one Jesus gave to his disciples, in what became known as the Lord's Prayer. It is found in the gospels of Matthew (6:9-13) and Luke (11:2-4). It should be clear that Jesus did not intend for his disciples merely to repeat verbatim the words

---

[12] For an idea of some of the writers and biographies that have stirred my heart the most see Gary S. Maxey, *Going Deeper With God* (Lagos: WATS Publications, 2020), "Discovering the Christian Classics," 47-54; "Discovering Christian Biography," 55-62; "Five Modern Mentors," 63-84.

of this model prayer, though that practice has made it the most widely offered prayer in history. Rather, Jesus was responding to his disciples' appeal to be taught to pray. By giving them the prayer he was suggesting basic contents of personal prayer: (1) begin with acknowledgement and worship of God himself, (2) pray for the advancement of God's kingdom through the spread of the gospel, (3) pray for our daily needs, (4) pray for forgiveness for our sins, and for our grace to forgive others, and (5) pray for victory over the evil one. Using that guide in our personal prayer time is still as valid today as it was when Jesus first gave it!

Another more modern yet time-honored guide for personal prayer is the use of the ACTS acronym, which shares similarities with the Lord's Prayer. The ACTS acronym advocates four general categories for personal prayers. First is ADORATION. It is healthy and edifying to always begin prayers with a focus on the worship of my Father God, on Jesus Christ and on the Holy Spirit. Taking time to worship God will pave the way for an effective prayer time. Expressing my love to God is one of the surest ways to maintain spiritual health and strength.

Second is CONFESSION. Coming before God with an awareness of my own shortcomings, of my utter dependence on God, and of areas of carelessness and failure encourages me to ask for daily forgiveness. This is not because I am the same rebellious person I was before I knew the Lord, but because I am still full of human faults and failures. I need the forgiveness of God every day of my life.

Third is THANKSGIVING. The marvel of God's forgiveness is that it is always available, and for that I must remain deeply thankful. The gifts of life, of health, of family, of friends, of community, of church, etc., are never to be taken for granted. God is worthy of thanks at every turn in my life.

Last comes SUPPLICATION. God loves it when I come into his presence with my petitions, though it is seldom appropriate to start on that note. A child always asking for favors from a parent and never expressing appreciation or love is not a balanced person and is not expressing a healthy relationship. But when love has been established, and when worship has predominated, God loves to hear the cries of his children asking for his intervention in their lives.

Whether you follow the pattern in the Lord's Prayer, in the ACTS paradigm or any other guide, it is important that our prayers be consistent and satisfying. Prayer is our very breath. It is one of the greatest secrets to our ministerial success.

John Hyde: A Man in Love with Jesus

One of the largely unsung heroes of a hundred years ago was an American missionary by the name of John Hyde. He became known even in his lifetime as "Praying Hyde." His gravestone bears the simple words, "Praying Hyde of India." He lived from 1865 to 1912. Hyde graduated from McCormick Theological Seminary in 1892 at the height of the Student Volunteer Movement, in a class of forty-six seniors of whom twenty-six were pledged to be missionaries.

Hyde sailed to India in late 1892. Opening a farewell letter from a friend after boarding his ship, he read, "I shall not cease praying for you, dear John, until you are filled with the Spirit." Hyde felt insulted and crushed the letter and threw it into a corner with anger, though he knew that the writer loved him dearly. However, after prayer, Hyde realized that the writer was correct, and he determined that whatever the cost he would be filled with the fulness of the Holy Spirit. For weeks he struggled, especially with one besetting sin, until at last, John Hyde experienced full deliverance and cleansing from his inner uncleanness.

Hyde spent a total of nineteen years in India. By his third year he began to nurture a heavy burden for revival. Gradually he became more focused on spending long hours, including whole nights, in prayer. After his only furlough back to the US in 1902, others joined him in intercession for revival, by forming the Punjab Prayer Union. In addition to their normal times of personal devotion, all agreed to pray for revival and for more of the Holy Spirit's power in their own lives and work, and to set apart a half hour for intercession daily as soon after noon as possible, praying for spiritual awakening.

A convention was called at Sialkot, India, in 1904, and repeated annually over the next six years. Year by year, God gave John Hyde a growing life of intercessory prayer, as well as a burden to lead a specific number of souls to Christ on a daily basis, until he was eventually seeing four daily converts. Those who knew John said his life was holiness manifested in Christlikeness and that his three outstanding characteristics were an ardent love for Jesus, passionate love for the Indian people among whom he worked, and loving affection for his fellow missionaries. His ministry was anointed with tears. Even today, the life of John Hyde continues to teach us that our devotional life, and especially our life of prayer, is a potential foundation for enormous spiritual success.[13]

---

[13]Wesley L. Duewel, *Heroes of the Holy Life* (Grand Rapids: Zondervan, 2002), Kindle loc 1304-1491. Basil Miller, *Praying Hyde: A Man of Prayer* (Grand Rapids: Zondervan, 1943).

HUMILITY/ BROKENNESS

The cultivation of a life of humility is of inestimable value for anyone who desires to have maximum success in Christian life and ministry. There is no amount of talent, hard work, financial backing or organizational skills that will ultimately come to the rescue of a man or woman who has given in to fleshly and spiritual pride. Pride is a killer. The Bible is quite clear on this issue: *"Pride goes before destruction, and a haughty spirit before a fall"* (Prov. 16:18).

In his letter to the Colossians, Paul describes the life and character of believers in these terms:

> *Therefore, as the elect of God, holy and beloved, put on tender mercies, kindness, humility, meekness, longsuffering; bearing with one another, and forgiving one another, if anyone has a complaint against another; even as Christ forgave you, so you also must do. But above all these things put on love, which is the bond of perfection"* (Col. 3:12-14).

I do not see any place in that definition for fleshly pride. The word "humility" in verse 12 means "lowliness of mind." In other words, true humility does not primarily involve outward actions. Rather, it describes our inner heart attitude. How do I see myself? We all know that I could easily put on a great outward show of humility but at the same time have unreasonable and unseemly exalted views of myself. Proverbs 23:7 says, *"as he thinks in his heart, so is he."*

I well remember the work of the Holy Spirit not long after my spiritual new birth in which he showed me my unChristlike attitude of superiority. At first, I did not realize it was there. I certainly would never have admitted it openly. However, I eventually could not deny that a very ungodly pride was there. The core of that attitude was that I believed I was better than others, more dedicated than others, more spiritual than others, etc. In those days I was still in my late teens, yet in my heart I felt I could do a better job of pastoring our church than my pastor, who was twice my age and who had been trained for the job. So, the real question here is how do I see myself in the secret recesses of my heart?

If we understand the nature of the new birth, we will quickly see that humility is essential for anyone coming to God for salvation. Jesus pointed this out to his disciples by comparing the proud Pharisee with the penitent tax collector who, *"standing afar off, would not so much as raise his eyes to heaven, but beat his breast, saying, 'God, be merciful to me a sinner!'"* (Luke 18:13). That is the attitude of humility that triggers great grace for God to unworthy sinners.

Yet it goes even further than that. Humility is necessary to get into the heavenly kingdom, but it is also necessary for anyone who would make progress and become great in the kingdom. Peter urged his fellow believers, *"Clothe yourselves, all of you, with humility"* (1 Pet. 5:5). It is also why Jesus taught his disciples: *"whoever desires to become great among you, let him be your servant. And whoever desires to be first among you, let him be your slave—just as the Son of Man did not come to be served, but to serve, and to give His life a ransom for many"* (Matt. 20:26-28).

Clearly, Jesus is our model when it comes to humility. That is why Christian leadership that is truly worthy of our calling does not leave any room for selfish ambition, pride, or self-justification and self-defense in the face of conflict.

To see the importance of humility we can also remember Jesus' first "beatitude" in Matthew 5: *"Blessed are the poor in spirit"* (Matt. 5:3). This is the humility that is absolutely essential for those who come to God as sinners seeking reconciliation and salvation. Only when we see our own poverty, wretchedness and inability to save ourselves can we receive God's forgiveness and salvation. We must never forget that the pathway to God always requires humility.

For many years my wife has been a champion of the Celebrate Recovery program initiated by the Saddleback Church in California, where Rick Warren is the founding pastor. The foundation of that program is based on eight principles drawn from Jesus' Beatitudes. The fourth principle relates to what I am talking about in this chapter:

"Openly examine and confess my faults to myself, to God, and to someone I trust."[14]

We must continually remember that humility is of equal importance as we continue our Christian journey. It is clear that the disciples of Jesus had some tough lessons to learn along this line. James and John wanted exalted seats next to Jesus, which angered their fellow disciples. All the disciples boasted that they would follow Jesus all the way to death. They found it hard to learn the lessons Jesus was trying to teach them about becoming a servant of all as the pathway to kingdom greatness. Jesus said, *"Whoever desires to become great among you, let him be your servant. And whoever desires to be first among you, let him be your slave"* (Matt. 20:26b-27).

I cannot think of any man in the scriptures whom we could properly admire as a truly great man who was not also humble. Perhaps it is possible for some to be regarded as great without humility, but if so, their greatness of necessity bears with it an unnecessary and diminishing burden. What we do know is that the Bible again and again extols the humble. Jesus modeled humility (Matt. 11:29). Moses was said to be *"more humble than any other person"* (Num. 12:3). Paul was a humble man (2 Cor. 10:1). Repeatedly we are all commanded to be clothed with humility (Eph. 4:2; 1 Pet. 3:8).

Regrettably, the commandment toward humility seems to be a difficult lesson for many church leaders in our own day. It appears that some of them wrongly view humility as

---

[14]John Baker, *Celebrate Recovery Africa: A Recovery Program Based on Eight Principles from the Beatitudes* (Grand Rapids: Zondervan, 1998), 11.

a weakness, believing that it may somehow diminish their reputation. The result is that in too many cases pride becomes the expected demeanor of leadership. Surely one of the most unrebuked sins in the Nigerian Church is pride. In some circles pride (not humility) is seen as a virtue, and not as the besetting, fatal sin it really is.

If you have difficulty learning this lesson, I strongly urge you to spend time studying the life of Jesus. The quickest way to understand the importance of humility as a hallmark of strength and good leadership is to contemplate Jesus' example. Not many would make the mistake of believing it is not good to follow the footsteps of Jesus. Peter said, *"Christ also suffered for us, leaving us an example, that you should follow His steps"* (1 Pet. 2:21). It is essential to ask what kind of example Jesus left with respect to humility.

I am sure you already know the answer. Jesus, despite being the Son of God, was one of the humblest men to walk the face of this earth. He knelt to wash the feet of his disciples (John 13:1-16). He constantly expressed his submission to the Heavenly Father. Paul says he *"made himself nothing by taking the very nature of a servant, and deliberately put the interests of others above his own"* (Phil. 2:3, 5ff).

As long as we live, we should remain challenged by the example of Jesus. Our inherited human nature is to be proud, and to resist those who oppose us. We find it all too easy to misjudge the motives of others and to quickly condemn those with whom we disagree. Understanding these natural tendencies should all the more encourage us to seek the deeper cleansing that enables us to more effectively be *"partakers of the divine nature"* (2 Pet. 1:4). When that happens, we will be able to exemplify Paul's admonition to Timothy, where he noted that *"a servant of the Lord must not quarrel but be gentle to all, able to teach, patient"* (2 Tim. 2:24).

May we all never forget that the cultivation of a spirit of humility is one of the great secrets of Christian success. We must continually learn new ways in which to serve others. When we do that, we are bringing more of God's help, or grace, into our lives. God gives grace to the humble, but he resists the proud (Prov. 3:34; 1 Pet. 5:5).

HUMILITY AND SELF-DENIAL

There is a close inter-connection between the Christian virtues of humility and self-denial. They are like Siamese twins. Wherever you find one, the other will also be present. Moreover, it is impossible for one to experience the deeper sanctification to which the Holy Spirit calls all true believers without being ushered into a life of progressively greater humility and self-denial. The self-denial that we see exemplified in the lives of the great saints of by-gone centuries include men such as St. Francis of Assisi, George Fox, John Wesley and William Booth.

What we see is that the work of the Holy Spirit in the life of those who have experienced the cleansing fulness of the Holy Spirit leads to a lowliness of spirit, a humbleness of mind, a deep self-denial and pure and holy love. Commissioner Samuel L. Brengle of the Salvation Army, who was another great exemplar of sanctified humility and self-denial, made these observations about self-denial:

> There are four kinds of self-denial. 1. There is compulsory self-denial, where we deny ourselves because we are forced to it by necessity. There is no virtue in this. 2. There is the more formal self-denial, where it is done purely as a form, because it is the fashion, and it would not be good taste or policy not to deny ourselves. There is no virtue in this. 3. There is a self-denial that springs from principle, where we deny ourselves because we know it is right, and we choose to do the right thing at whatever cost. This is well-pleasing to the Lord and will surely have its reward. 4. But best of all, there is a self-denial that is joyous, springs from love – love to God and man. This is its own reward.[15]

BROKENNESS

A Christian quality that was talked about fifty years ago in Nigeria, but that seems to have been forgotten in more recent years is brokenness. It was also a hallmark during the great East African Revival, the longest-lasting revival that ever visited this continent, and arguably the greatest revival in Christian history. However, I am not sure most contemporary Christian audiences would know what brokenness is about. Usually when we think of broken things, we regard them as no longer needed and to be

---

[15]Samuel L. Brengle, "Four Kinds of Self-Denial," *War Cry* [NY] (April 14, 1917). 13, quoted in R. David Rightmire, *Op cit*, 146.

tossed out. We reject damaged goods, often including people as well.

Strangely, though, God tells us in his word that *"The LORD is close to the brokenhearted and saves those who are crushed in spirit"* (Ps. 34:18). Apparently unlike us, God values "damaged goods." People who have reached a breaking point in their lives are often far more ready to seek the face of God. On the other hand, when we have not yet experienced the trauma of seeing our world crumble around us, we too often remain deaf to the quiet voice of the Holy Spirit. That is why often when I see a man or woman of over-weaning pride, which they themselves usually do not even acknowledge, I say to myself, "There goes a person who has never been truly broken."

I have discovered that God can use a wide variety of means to deal with the things in our lives that need to be broken (pride, stubbornness, sinful habits, etc.). He sometimes uses deep and unexpected trauma. This can include near-death experiences, the death of a close loved one, the shattering trauma of divorce, total financial collapse, etc. People who experience these shattering things are sometimes brought to a breaking point in their spirit in which they experience a healthy brokenness of spirit.

It is also possible for others to be brought low in the presence of God through the direct probing of the Holy Spirit. For those who are brave enough to hold themselves before the blazing light of God, he can use the deep and often painful probing of the Holy Spirit to show us the reality of our inner self.

About twenty years ago Chinyere Madugba published a book entitled *Brokenness: An Inevitable Experience for Spiritual Significance.*[16] In that book she talks about the nature and the importance of cultivating this important Christian attitude. It is a book that I wish could be read all over Nigeria.

Another man who grasped the importance of brokenness was A. W. Tozer. He once said, "It is doubtful whether God can bless a man greatly until He has hurt him deeply." I can assure you those wounds of the Holy Spirit are priceless. The Apostle Paul knew about it. It is no doubt what compelled him to write, *"I am crucified with Christ"* (Gal. 2:20).

I don't need to remind us that crucifixion is not pleasant. It is not a matter of passively waiting for God to zap us with some kind of ecstasy. Paul said further, *"I bear in my body the marks of the Lord Jesus"* (Gal. 6:17). Both Tozer and Paul understood what it means to experience spiritual brokenness.

It is a pity that there are too many in positions of leadership who have never been broken. They have never experienced what it is to die to their own pride and ambitions and sense of self-exaltation and to learn how to quickly and *instinctively* take the lower seat, to never fret when they go unrecognized, to in honor prefer others over themselves, and to patiently suffer unjust rebukes, insults

---

[16]Chinyere Gloria Madugba, *Brokenness: An Inevitable Experience for Spiritual Significance* (Port Harcourt: Spiritual Life Outreach Publications, 2002).

and injuries. The world needs more broken people, and there is no reason you and I cannot be among them.

One of the greatest saints of God I ever worked with in Nigeria was Sam Nwosu, who flamed out for God at a young age, thirty years ago. At the close of a highly energetic and fruitful evangelistic ministry he went to be with Jesus suddenly in a horrific head-on road accident. Sam was one of the most talented and accomplished and yet one of the humblest men I ever knew.

Sam and I ministered together in revival campaigns, at times sleeping in the same bed. He was a man of unceasing prayer. His example still inspires me today. He suffered unjust rebukes and accusations and received it all in the spirit of Christ. Sam knew what humility is about, and the fruits of his ministry are still visible today.

On the opposite side, we have seen Nigerian leaders who have embarrassed themselves and all the rest of us by their lack of Christian humility. One of them at the head of a large church ignominiously disgraced himself through his sexual immorality, and then openly and brazenly divorced his wife. He defended and excused his blatantly immoral actions by simply boasting that as a "man of God" he was immune from censure. He was quoted as saying to his people, in the context of his own egregious sins:

> You have to understand something about a man of God. A man of God is not just someone who worships God or preaches God. A man of God is handpicked by God, set on course by God. If you

study the scriptures, you will not find one man of God go against God, sinning against God.

On the other hand, people who have experienced brokenness are usually not difficult to spot, though they never seek to deliberately draw attention to themselves. They have a tenderness of spirit and a sense of unpretentious humility about them. They are not harsh-spirited people but are gentle like Jesus. They have been broken, and as a result they know how to deal gently with those who are in pain.

MEEKNESS IS NOT WEAKNESS

I am sure there are some who shy away from the concept of humility because they believe it must be associated with weakness. They have bought a false idea that to be humble means we do not stand up for righteousness and justice. Instead, we allow ourselves to be swayed back and forth by moral evil. That is not an accurate picture of Christian humility.

Jesus was a humble man, and so much so that the saying was (following the prophesy of Isaiah, as quoted in Matt. 12:19-20), *"He will not quarrel or cry out; no one will hear his voice in the streets. A bruised reed he will not break, and a smoldering wick he will not snuff out."* In other words, this Jesus was not ranting and raving in a loud voice. He was gentle in spirit and demeanor. Paul urged the Philippians to follow that kind of example (Phil. 2:5ff).

To interpret this as weakness on the part of Jesus would be a huge mistake. In the same prophesy quoted by Matthew, it says of Jesus that, *"He will proclaim justice to the nations. . . . till he has brought justice through to victory"* (vv. 18, 20). Jesus was meek and Jesus was humble, but Jesus was not a weak man. Neither are we when we are clothed with proper Christian humility.

RESPONDING TO MISTREATMENT

One of the greatest marks of Christian humility is our ability to respond to mistreatment, misunderstandings and false accusations in a mature and Christlike manner. How do we respond when we are slighted, when we are overlooked, when we are underappreciated, or even when we are seriously mistreated and falsely slandered and accused? It is when we feel the sting of self-pity and realize that we have been mistreated that pride usually wants to jump to our defense.

The greatest opportunities for the cultivation of humility are often those moments or epochs in our lives when we are dealt with undeserved blows.

We know from the writings of the Apostle Paul that this was his own lot. In recounting some of the dangers and near-death experiences he went through, recorded in 2 Corinthians 11, he includes *"perils among my own countrymen,"* and *"perils among false brethren."* He told Timothy that he *"suffered trouble as an evildoer, even to the point of chains"* (2 Tim. 2:9). Paul knew what it was to be falsely accused and to suffer all kinds of mistreatment and misunderstanding.

As I look back over my life, I can see several such painful periods. As a young man in my early 20s, I was put into a position of leadership that was probably more than I should have been expected to handle. When I then faced an impossible situation involving the moral failure on the part of an older missionary colleague, I was forced to become the sacrificial lamb. I was ignominiously fired and sent away in undeserved shame. I had done nothing to merit such unjust, harsh and embarrassing treatment.

Yet now the question was how I was going to respond to such mistreatment. Should I jump to my own defense? Should I make wide protestations of my innocence? Should I threaten to take legal action against the obvious injustice?

I thank God that in that difficult hour he gave me the grace to remain silent, and to allow God to deal with the situation. I have never regretted that. It is possible that even today some may still misunderstand and misjudge what happened, yet my soul is free, and my conscience is clear.

No one knows better than myself that I do not deserve the mercies of God. It is a miracle that God loves me. All of the good things I may have done in my life have not earned me even five minutes in heaven. Therefore, I can afford to let go of those painful things in my life where I may have suffered seemingly undeserved blows.

I can recount other episodes in my life where I have faced unjust and painful mistreatment, even during my decades of missionary service in Nigeria. In 1989 my family and I were mercilessly chased out of Port Harcourt, under threat of deportation, which we narrowly escaped. In 1993 I was harshly vilified by those who had earlier been my leaders. In these and other cases I have been seriously mistreated and deeply wounded, even though not always without at least a degree of failure on my own part.

The plain truth is that all of us are likely to receive mistreatment from time to time in our Christian walk. We will be slighted, overlooked, lied about and underappreciated. Yet here are at least a few of the things I have learned over the years about response to mistreatment.

First and foremost is that I cannot imagine how I could have sailed so victoriously through my trials-by-fire without the foundation of the consecration and deeper sanctification I experienced as an eighteen-year-old. Through that experience God showed me clearly that my life would be one of severe trial, and *I freely accepted it as the will of God!* As I confronted each painful trial there was an underlying confidence that God was in control and that what I was experiencing is what I had already accepted in my spirit years before. That is the power of the Holy Spirit at work in a consecrated and sanctified life.

Second, I have deliberately chosen to not dwell on the past. Do not allow yourself to be consumed with anger or regret or to curl up in a ball and bemoan your fate. Your pain will be real, but you must not allow it to simmer or boil over in your soul. Therefore, move forward quickly.

To help you stop fixating on the past, as soon as possible find out what the next step is in your life. I know what it is to find the carpet pulled out from under my feet and suddenly have all my dreams and plans dashed to pieces. It is an unpleasant and shocking thing. To see long-cherished dreams terminated with no chance for revival can be devastating.

Yet I have learned to always quickly move on, without wasting time looking back. God still has something for me to do, even if I cannot continue to do the thing my heart has been set on. I am still alive. I am still God's man with more assignments ahead of me. I have therefore learned deeply to never let past failure or defeat define me. You can do the same.

Third, I have been slow to defend myself. Here is where too many of us make major mistakes. We give in to the natural compulsion to tell our side of the story. We do not like the sharp sting of being misjudged, misunderstood, and lied about. We therefore feel compelled to talk, talk, and talk. We want to write letters, to send emails, to make phone calls, or to rush to social media to defend ourselves. I can tell you that is almost never the right direction to go. Do not quarrel with your adversaries. Let God handle it.

Fourth, I have not allowed bitterness to take root in my heart. In that great chapter in Ephesians where Paul urges us to not give Satan a foothold (Eph. 4), one of the things he urges us is to get rid of all bitterness (v. 31). There is nothing that will drag us down quite as quickly as a spirit of bitterness. It is the kind of attitude that eats like an ugly canker and that has the ability to bring our entire life to a halt. Therefore, when you feel the temptation to bitterness find something positive and uplifting on which to focus. Make a determination to stamp out bitterness from your life.

Finally, after an adequate period of time I have sought for reconciliation. Usually when mistreatment is still fresh in our minds and hearts it is not possible to quickly rush in and bring about reconciliation. Yet sooner or later tempers will cool down. Reason will become clearer. That is the point where anyone who is truly in love with Jesus will have a desire to seek and find reconciliation.

Sometimes reconciliation is not possible, either because the parties are no longer alive or because they just do not want to consider reconciliation. Yet I pray none of us will be content to go to our graves without making a reasonable attempt to come to reconciliation. That is the true spirit of Christian humility.

The dynamics involved in responding to misunderstandings and mistreatment bear significant similarities with how we respond to any other kind of suffering in life. We know that God has great healing power, but we also know that for reasons best known to himself at times he allows his children to experience even prolonged suffering. We can be assured that victory over physical suffering is more than possible through the power of the indwelling Spirit!

Early in his dynamic and fruitful ministry career, Samuel Brengle received a fierce blow to his head from a large brick thrown by a ruffian. It nearly took his life. For eighteen long months he was laid up in prolonged recovery. Here is how years later he expressed triumph even through suffering:

> The Lord enables the man filled with the Spirit to thus triumph over suffering . . . by giving the soul a sweet, constant and unshaken assurance through faith: *First*, that it is freely and fully accepted in Christ. *Second*, that whatever suffering comes, it is measured, weighed and permitted by love infinitely tender, and guided by wisdom that cannot err. *Third*, that however difficult it may be to explain suffering now, it is nevertheless *one* of the "all things" which "work together for good to them that love God," and that in a "little while" it will not only be swallowed up in ineffable blessedness and glory, but that in some way it is actually helping to work out "a far more exceeding and eternal weight of glory." *Fourth*, that though the furnace has been heated seven times hotter than was wont, yet "the Form . . . like unto the Son of God" is walking with us in the fire. . . . This is faith's triumph over the worst the world can offer through the blessed fullness of the indwelling Comforter.[17]

---

[17]Rightmire, *Op cit,* 146-147.

Samuel Brengle: A Broken Vessel

One of the great examples of Christian humility was the man I have just quoted: Commissioner Samuel L. Brengle. He rose to widespread fame while in the service of the Salvation Army. As a young man, however, there was nothing about the education of Brengle that was intended or likely to lead him into a life of service one day in the Salvation Army. He was born in 1860, and as a young man surrendered himself to God and began to move toward a life of ministerial service within the Methodist Church. At that stage most people who knew the Salvation Army saw them as a somewhat rag-tag group working with the lower classes and operating far below the dignity of the more established churches.

While still in his early 20s, Brengle became convinced of his need for holiness of heart and life, especially after listening to Dwight L. Moody's preaching about the Baptism of the Holy Spirit. Through much prayer, study of the scripture and the reading of holiness writings from John Wesley, John Fletcher, Hannah Whittal Smith, Catherine Booth and others, Brengle's hunger for a personal experience and life of holiness greatly increased.

For several weeks he earnestly sought for this spiritual blessing. He attended holiness meetings, yet without clear results. "I sought the blessing and was richly blessed, but I did not get the blessing and the blessing I did received leaked out," he later wrote. That was when he began to discover that what he had been seeking was primarily for greater empowerment for service, rather than for the purification of heart and life by the indwelling presence of the Spirit of Christ. He had hoped to get something that would make him a great preacher, but he eventually confessed, "I was seeking the Holy Spirit that I might use Him, rather than that He might use me."

At that point Brengle came under deep conviction for his sinful pride and self-centeredness. As he later testified:

> I saw the humility of Jesus and my pride; the meekness of Jesus and my tempter; the lowliness of Jesus and my ambition; the purity of Jesus and my unclean heart; the selflessness of Jesus and my selfishness; the trust and faith of Jesus and my doubts and unbelief; the holiness of Jesus and my unholiness. I got my eyes off everybody but Jesus and myself, and I came to loathe myself. I ceased to want to be a bishop. I was willing to take the littlest church and the meanest appointment that could be found. I was willing to appear a big blunder and failure if He would only cleanse me and dwell in me.

At that point Brengle made a far more complete surrender to God than he had ever before known. He was able to pray: "Lord, I wanted to be an eloquent preacher, but if by stammering and stuttering I can bring greater glory to Thee than by eloquence, then let me stammer and stutter!"

Having made a total consecration to God, through the prompting of the Holy Spirit Brengle was enabled to exercise faith for the experience of the deeper sanctification that had eluded him for many long months. On January 9, 1885, he received a flood of peace in his soul that set the tone for the next fifty-plus years. In fact, more than fifty years later he wrote:

> The glory of that blessed experience has not faded through all the years. It was more than an experience—it was more than a blessing—it was the Blesser Himself that came in tender love and everlasting mercy and great kindness to dwell in my poor heart, making it clean, keeping it clean and promising never to lever nor forsake me. Hallelujah!

Brengle's transitioned to the Salvation Army during years when they were looked down on by many other religious organizations because of their simplicity, their relatively less-educated "cadets" and "officers," and their noisy parades. It was not easy. By this time Brengle was theologically trained at one of the leading theological schools in America. Nevertheless, he was determined to offer his services to the lowly Salvation Army. He traveled to London and presented himself to the head of the Army, General William Booth, who received him with skepticism. Years later Brengle described what happened:

> My second day at the Salvation Army training school, they sent me to black half a cartload of dirty boots. The devil came to me, and reminded me that

I had graduated from a university, had attended a leading theological school, had been pastor of a metropolitan church, had just left evangelistic work in which I saw hundreds seeking the Savior, and that now I was only blacking boots for a lot of ignorant lads. But I reminded my old enemy of the example of my Lord, and he left me, and that little cellar was changed into one of heaven's anterooms, and my Lord visited me there.[18]

It was that example of humility that enabled Brengle to succeed. Later, after his return to America, he faced the shame and scorn of former classmates and teachers because of his identity with the rag-tag Salvationists, yet he sailed through in the will of God. He lived on for fifty years to bless millions, both inside and outside of the Salvation Army. To this day we can thank God for the godly example of humility that was given to us through the life and ministry of Samuel L. Brengle.

---

[18]Samuel Logan Brengle, *Helps to Holiness*, 38, as quoted in *Take Time to be Holy*, loc. 2214; R. David Rightmire, *Sanctified Sanity: The Life and Teaching of Samuel Logan Brengle* (Alexandria, VA: Crest Books, 2003), 13-19.

TRANSPARENCY

Ever since I arrived in Africa nearly forty years ago, I have observed that my African brothers and sisters have a general tendency to be more reticent, more cautious, more close-mouthed and more self-protective than I was accustomed to as a child. By contrast, I have observed that Africans often look on Americans like me as too talkative, too self-disclosing and even dangerously over-informative, especially with strangers.

In some of my trips to the immigration office, for example, my African friends have warned me to only narrowly answer whatever questions I am asked, and to not offer unsolicited information. I am sure they had more wisdom than I. Yet eventually I also came to the conclusion that my African friends were descended from many generations of people who lived with a sense of caution about other clans or ethnic groups around them, and even many times factions within their own kindred, that might use any possible advantage to betray or undo them.

What I am talking about here is transparency. I believe an essential quality of holy living is transparency. I cannot for a second imagine that Jesus of Nazareth was anything but open, transparent, and candid in all his interactions with those around him. I can't believe he hid his real feelings or put on a deliberate mask to disguise himself.

The word for "hypocrite" in the New Testament is the word for "actor." Literally, it refers to someone "wearing a mask," meaning someone who pretends to be what he is not. It means thinking one thing in my mind but saying the opposite with my mouth. The Bible labels such behavior as sinful.

Isaiah complained about the people of God, for example, saying, *"these people draw near with their mouths and honor Me with their lips, but have removed their hearts far from Me"* (Is. 29:13). Jesus used those words to refer to the Jewish leaders (Matt. 15:8-9). He talked about the same issue in the Sermon on the Mount, warning against criticizing others from a position of presumed innocence or self-righteousness. He said,

> *And why do you look at the speck in your brother's eye, but do not consider the plank in your own eye? Or how can you say to your brother, 'Let me remove the speck from your eye'; and look, a plank is in your own eye? Hypocrite! First remove the plank from your own eye, and then you will see clearly to remove the speck from your brother's eye* (Matt. 7:3-5).

What we must strive toward as mature believers, no matter what our cultural background may be, is to be men and women of transparency. We are not pretenders. We have turned our backs on former lives of duplicity and deceit, which we have all known in the past. We are guarding against unworthy motives. Our lives are an open book to everyone around us.

If we live that kind of life our spouse who lives with us 24/7 will be at ease and will not be wondering if we are constantly hiding things. We will never have to find ourselves suddenly covering up what we are doing, saying, reading or looking at when someone unexpected suddenly appears. We would not be embarrassed if Jesus himself were to suddenly appear before us in all of his glory. That is what happens when we are truly transparent. One of the ways John expressed this was by writing, *"as He is, so are we in this world"* (1 John 4:17).

I also love what Paul told the Corinthians on this topic. *"Therefore, since we have this ministry, as we have received mercy, we do not lose heart. But we have renounced the hidden things of shame, not walking in craftiness nor handling the word of God deceitfully, but by manifestation of the truth commending ourselves to every man's conscience in the sight of God"* (2 Cor. 4:2). Here he puts his finger on the fact that we can only walk in transparency if we have first renounced those things in our lives that have brought or are still bringing shame. You cannot be a man or woman of transparency if you have not cleaned house! Everything that is unlike Jesus or unworthy of Jesus must be swept out and gone. Often, people who are not transparent are people who have something to hide.

Paul also says we must stop walking in craftiness. I do not know all Paul had in his mind, but it certainly refers to people who have impure motives about what they are doing. They therefore cannot be open and honest about what they are doing and why they are doing it. Worse yet, they may use the word of God in a deceitful manner. They take up the word of God and use it for their own base or inferior motives. Posing as Bible experts they are in truth only seeking with veiled motives to achieve ends about which they cannot speak openly and plainly. They are, in other words, deceivers. God is not happy with deceivers. It is the trademark of Satan himself.

Let me tell you a secret. I have personally prayed these words of Paul in 2

Corinthians 4:2 *many scores of times* in my private prayers as a renewed pledge to God, promising God that I will continue to be a man of transparency. You, too, can do that. I would love to have the continuing commendation from God that Jesus gave regarding Nathanael in John 1:47. *"Jesus saw Nathanael coming toward Him, and said of him, 'Behold, an Israelite indeed, in whom is no deceit!'"* I hope that describes you, too!

One of the remarkable stories in the New Testament that warns us about what can happen when we are not transparent is the story of Ananias and Sapphira in Acts 5. Here was a couple who at a strategic point in their lives abandoned transparency and pretended to be more spiritual than they really were. I assume that they must have been well respected members of the Early Church, with strong dedication. They arose to the challenge of selling their possessions in order to put the proceeds into the common treasurer. However, in a moment of deception, abandoning the open transparency with which the Church was operating, they pretended they had given everything when in reality they had not.

What followed was shocking. It was swift and dramatic. The point is that God does not favor dishonesty and deception. He values transparency. He honors us when we see ourselves as we really are, who are willing to confess our shortcomings and needs to him, and who are prepared to receive his help to become the person he wants us to be.

For me to stand up in front of an audience and talk about how great it is to live for Jesus and how wonderful it is to be a victorious believer when I know I am living in secret sin and my life is messed up is an abomination to God. On the other hand, to be honest and open before my people about some of my struggles in striving to live a victorious and godly life can be very honoring to God if I do it in a wise and humble way. Both God and people value leaders who are honest and open. On the contrary, those who live with pretense and are not ready to be transparent are doomed to shallowness and defeat.

Does your life hold up to close scrutiny? Could Jesus say of you what he said of Nathanael? "He is a man or woman in whom is no deceit?" If you and I are to be men and women of holiness that is the standard we cannot and must not miss.

Let's ask ourselves some questions:

- ❖ Are we transparent about financial matters? Do we misrepresent, misreport or mislead others about those issues? This is particularly crucial issue between husbands and wives. It may not be wrong for wives to have discretionary spending which they do not have to report detail-by-detail to their husbands, but it is always wrong to lie or to deceive. Let us be careful!

- ❖ Are we transparent about our relationships with the opposite sex? Is there any hint of hidden infatuation or attraction that should be shunned and forsaken? It is paramount for all of us to keep the inner chambers of our hearts and minds completely free before the Lord, and before others.

- ❖ Are we transparent about what we read and what we look at? Anything that crosses our desk or is involved in our reading should be above reproach. Job said that he made a covenant *with his eyes. "I have made a covenant with my eyes; why then should I look upon a young woman?"* (Job 31:1). We all know that the possibility of "looking upon a young woman" today is infinitely greater than in Job's day. It is paramount for us to maintain transparency and integrity in this area.

- ❖ Are we transparent about where we go on the internet? Nothing has transformed our lives in modern times more than the internet, for better and also for worse. That is why I have made sure for many years that I have an internet filter that not only blocks objectionable sites but that sends a report every two weeks to my wife, so she is privy to everything I do on the internet. Why? Because I want to be transparent, and I want her to know that I am guarding where I go on the internet.

❖ Are we transparent about where we get our resources? I am talking about *plagiarism*, where I copy the works of others word-for-word without giving them credit, and present to others as my own work what has been toiled over and produced by others. It is not wrong for me as a preacher or as a writer to utilize such thoughts and outlines and other resources from other preachers and writers, but where I use large blocks of material without giving credit to the original thinker, I lack precious and necessary transparency.

When I was a child, we used to sing a chorus that has never left me, even in my senior years: "O, be careful little eyes what you see. For the Father up above is looking down in love. O be careful little eyes what you see." The key there for all of us is to remember that God is looking on. He is the one before whom we shall all stand one day in judgment. If we have learned to practice transparency in our life journey it will stand us in good stead when we appear before the throne of God.

Akanu Ibiam: A Man of Integrity

One of the great privileges of my life is to have known well a man of great integrity, Sir Elder Dr. Francis Akanu Ibiam. He was born in Unwana-Afikpo, now Ebonyi state on November 29, 1906, and died in December 1995, at the age of 89. Dr. Ibiam, who was also called 'Nna-anyi-ukwu' meaning great father or father-of-all in local Unwana parlance, his hometown, was a distinguished medical missionary who was appointed Governor of Eastern Region, Nigeria from December 1960 until January 1966, during Nigeria's First Republic.

Dr. Ibiam told me that at age nine, while on a visit to Calabar, he saw the famed Scottish missionary Mary Slessor, not long before her death. As a child he schooled at Hope Waddell Training Institution, Calabar, where he later because the first African principal. His studies finally took him to St. Andrews University in Scotland, where we became a medical doctor.

Akanu Ibiam returned from Scotland and immediately applied to become a missionary doctor of the Church of Scotland in the hinterland of eastern Nigeria, after turning down lucrative offers of government employment. For around twenty years he worked tirelessly building up hospitals, evangelizing and ministering to the sick and dying. He established Abiriba hospital in 1936-1945. He later superintended mission hospitals at Itu and Uburu.

Dr. Ibiam throughout his lifetime was never ordained as a minister of a church but was elected and ordained an elder of the Presbyterian church. He was knighted by Queen Elizabeth in 1951 for his work as a medical missionary of the Church of Scotland. He was president of the Christian Council of Nigeria between 1955–1958. In 1957, he was appointed principal of Hope Waddell Institute where he faithfully upheld discipline and academic hard work.

He was a selfless leader and had a liberal heart. He equitably disbursed economic wealth and allocations meant for the region. He was also a leader who considered Nigeria and principally Igboland as his home. Dr. Ibiam was unmistakably referred to as "the soul of Biafra nation" during and after the Nigeria-Biafra civil war.

He was also not narrow minded by cultural differences. Even in marriage, he chose to marry a Yoruba woman, Lady Olayinka, from the great Sesegbon's family of Lagos state, a complete exhibition of oneness and true nationalism that was lacking in the country then.

Dr. Ibiam was a selfless leader and a man of genuine humility. He had a liberal heart. As the Governor of Eastern Nigeria, he disbursed economic wealth and allocations meant for the region in a fair and open manner. He never discriminated against people on any ground. In fact, he took care and ensured better well-being of 'outsiders' than his own people and sited a lot of developmental projects outside his locality to create that sense of belonging among people.

I got to know Dr. Ibiam during the final five years of his life, during which time he accepted appointment as the first chancellor of West Africa Theological Seminary. I became a regular visitor at his home in Unwana, where he spent his last days. I discovered that he had lived a life of transparency and had absolutely refused to enrich himself from public coffers.

In his service as our chancellor, Akanu Ibiam and I traveled on various occasions in the interests of the seminary. I shall never forget one day as I found myself sitting with him in the large throne room of the Esama of Benin. As we waited for the man of royalty to join us, we were seated opposite a group of a half dozen or so regally clothed Muslim leaders.

Suddenly I realized that these Muslims were talking about Dr. Ibiam, and as they talked, I overheard one of them saying, in a rather loud voice, "Kai! How I wish this man were a Muslim!" Then he went on to tell a story buttressing why he had made that comment.

As we sat there, this Muslim leader recounted a story that had spread far and wide about Dr. Ibiam. Prior to the outbreak of the Nigerian Civil War Ibiam had risen to become the first Lay President of the World Council of Churches. His integrity and transparency were known and respected all over the world.

At some point Ibiam succeeded in securing a substantial loan from the World Council of Churches for certain humanitarian needs in eastern Nigeria. But before the project could be carry out fully, quite unexpectedly Nigeria descended into the chaos of civil war. For thirty long and painful months eastern Nigeria—now transformed into Biafra—was ravaged by a struggle that eventually cost not less than two million lives. The devastation beggared description.

It was at the end of that brutal war that Akanu Ibiam finally made his way back to the World Council of Church headquarters, where to the stunned amazement of virtually everyone he returned to the leaders the unused portion of the loan given years before. It was that act of transparency and honesty that prompted our Muslim brother to say, "Kai! How I wish this man were a Muslim!" He knew that the kind of transparency that Ibiam was exemplifying is at best very rare.

However, that is the kind of transparency that any of us can and should be displaying. It is not something super-human. I knew Akanu Ibiam well enough to know that he was not a perfect man, yet I also knew that he was a man of sterling character, steadfast Christian discipline, with a commitment to scripture and prayer. He was a man of transparent integrity.[19]

---

[19]"Akanu Ibiam: Portrait of a Forgotten Statesman," *News Eye*, 24Nov2013; D. C. Nwafo, *Born to Serve: The Biography of Dr. Akanu Ibiam* (Ibadan: Macmillan Nigeria, 1988).

Jonathan Goforth: A Man of Transparency

There is one more man whose life of transparency bears notice. Jonathan Goforth was a Canadian Presbyterian who was used mightily of God in revivals in China and Korea in the early years of the 20th Century. Under Goforth's itinerating revival preaching, again and again God visited stoically unemotional Chinese with sweeping waves of repentance and open tears and confession. If you have not read the book that chronicles much of those revivals, *"By My Spirit,"* I appeal to you to try to get it and read it.

I want to quote at some length what Goforth shared later about his need to be totally transparent personally before God could use him as an instrument of revival for the Chinese.

In the autumn of 1906, having felt depressed for some time by the cold and fruitless condition of my out-stations, I was preparing to set out on a tour to see what could be done to revive them. There was a matter, however, between the Lord and myself, that had to be straightened out before He could use me. . . . There was a difference between a brother missionary and myself. I honestly felt that I was in the right. (Such, of course, is very human.) At any rate, the pressure from the Spirit was quite plain. It was that I should go and make that thing straight. I kept answering back to God that the fault was the other man's, not mine; that it was up to him to come to me, not for me to go to him.

The pressure continued. "But Lord, he came to my study and in tears confessed his fault. So, isn't the thing settled?" "You hypocrite!" I seemed to hear Him say, "you know you are not loving each other as brethren, as I commanded you to." Still I held out. The fault was the other man's, I kept insisting; surely, therefore, I couldn't be expected to do anything about it. Then came the final word, "If you don't straighten this thing out before you go on that trip, you must expect to fail. I can't go with you." That humbled me. I did not feel easy about going on that difficult tour without His help. Well I knew that by myself I would be like one beating the air.

The night before I was to start out on my trip, I had to lead the prayer-meeting for the Chinese Christians. All the way out to the church the pressure continued: "Go and straighten this thing out, so that I may go with you tomorrow." Still I wouldn't yield. I started the meeting. It was all right while they were singing a hymn and during the reading of the Scripture. But as soon as I opened my lips in prayer, I became confused, for all the time the Spirit kept saying: "You hypocrite! Why don't you straighten this thing out?" I became still more troubled while delivering the short prayer-address. Finally, when about half-way through my talk, the burden became utterly intolerable and I yielded. "Lord," I promised in my heart, "as soon as this meeting is over, I'll go and make that matter right."

Instantly something in the audience seemed to snap. My Chinese hearers couldn't tell what was going on in my heart; yet in a moment the whole atmosphere was changed. Upon the meeting being thrown open for prayer, one after another rose to their feet to pray, only to break down weeping. For almost twenty years we missionaries had been working among the Honanese, and had longed in vain to see a tear of penitence roll down a Chinese cheek.

It was late that might when the meeting closed. As soon as I could get away, I hastened over to the house of my brother missionary, only to find that the lights were out and the whole family were in bed. Not wishing to disturb them I went back to my home. But the difficulty was settled. Next morning, before daybreak, I was on my way to the first out-station. The results of that tour far exceeded anything that I had dared hope for. At each place the spirit of judgment was made manifest. Wrongs were righted and crooked things were made straight. At one place I was only able to spend a single night, but that night all present broke down. In the following year one out-station more than doubled its numbers; to another fifty-four members were added, and to another eighty-eight.[20]

---

[20]Jonathan Goforth, *"By My Spirit"* (Minneapolis: Bethany Fellowship, Inc., 1943), 24-25.

Jonathan Goforth went on to see many incredible breakthroughs in revival, even in places where his fellow missionaries swore that nothing like revival could ever happen among their stoic and emotionally rigid people. What we are seeing here are the fruits of transparency. Goforth was willing to be totally open and honest with God, and to make things right with his fellow missionaries, even on points that some might consider trivial.

What about you? Are you a man or woman of transparency? Have you renounced the hidden things of dishonesty that have lurked beneath the surface? God can help all of us to be people of sterling transparency!

MAINTAINING PRODUCTIVE WORK HABITS

Our Creator God provided for human beings the most incredibly regulated planet imaginable for our comfort and survival. It is true that human beings have learned to survive in a huge range of environments all over the globe, yet we must acknowledge that he made our bodies and this planet Earth so that they are suited for mutual survival.

The result is that all of us have at our disposal twenty-four hours in a day in which to order our living. Unlike our ancestors, we moderns have learned to artificially regulate the light and darkness in which we live so that we are not forced to order our activities so strictly around the rising and setting of the sun. We have also become much better at regulating the temperature and humidity in which we live so that we can conserve our energy more effectively. We have invented means of transportation that enable us to turn journeys formerly requiring days, weeks or even months into hours or minutes. Yet after all is said and done, there are still only twenty-four hours in a day, and either 365 or 366 days in a year.

One of the important measures of success in our Christian life is learning how to order and master our habits. We are creatures of habit. We do not easily tolerate chaos and confusion. Our health and well-being depend on regularity. People who have been imprisoned in solitary confinement testify that one of the most fundamental secrets to their physical and mental survival is to quickly take steps to regulate themselves. They learn quickly that in order to maintain sanity they cannot succumb to helplessness and despair. Rather, they must find ways to begin to establish routines and habits in which they as much as possible become masters of their own lives, even while incarcerated in solitary confinement.

Are you determined to succeed in life? Do you aspire to be a winner? Are you desirous of coming out at the top of your profession and being the *best* that God can make you? If so, you must be a person of high discipline and maximally productive work habits.

YOU CANNOT START TOO EARLY

When do champions of productive work habits get started? The answer should be obvious: sooner rather than later. The truth is that I was enormously blessed by being born in a family of high disciplinarians. I come from a long line of highly disciplined ancestors, for which I thank God. Not everyone has had that advantage, but if you have then you should pause and thank God.

Some of my earliest memories are of seeing six charts taped to the wall of our family bathroom. There was one for each child in the family, no matter our age. Each chart had a name at the top, and below were a range of ten or more age-appropriate daily responsibilities that had to be carried out by that child. Every day we had to indicate on the chart if our task was completed or not. The charts were replaced every month. Appropriate rewards were given for those who did well. For younger children brushing teeth, combing hair, sweeping the floor, and tidying their bed were common tasks. Older children had study assignments. *Everyone* had Bible passages to read and specific scriptures to be committed to memory.

If you grew up with the inculcation of positive habits, you should thank God. If you did not, you should at least ensure that you break the cycle in your family by ensuring that your own children learn strict discipline from yourself. Family rules and regulations are incredibly important. Learning to keep to time and to not be late for appointments should become a life-long habit. Being meticulously accurate and honest with money should be a fixed habit.

However, no matter how you started in life it is never too late to develop productive work habits. Even if you have spent most of your adult life without adequate discipline you can make a big difference in the remaining years of your life by becoming a more disciplined steward of your time and resources.

REGULATE YOURSELF

When we were younger, as children, probably all of us lived in environments that were characterized by some degree of regulation. Some of us were under more strict discipline than others, but all of us knew what it was to be required to get out of bed on time in the morning, get to school on time, fulfill our family responsibilities as assigned to us, etc. We were regulated by others. Frankly, some of us (probably most of us) looked forward to that future time when we would "be our own boss." There is something potentially unpleasant or chafing about being under the ruling hand of others. Most of us relish the idea of personal freedom.

Paul uses an interesting analogy along these lines in referring to the role played by the Old Testament law. He knew that the law was a *regulator*. Listen to how he put it: *"Therefore the law was our <u>tutor</u> to bring us to Christ, that we might be justified by faith. But after faith has come, we are no longer under a tutor. For you are all sons of God through faith in Christ Jesus"* (Gal. 3:24-26). The word "tutor" there is not very explicit in our English language. The footnote in my NKJV translation says about that word: "In a household, the guardian responsible for the care and discipline of the children."

The Greek word is *pedagogos*. Very specifically, it referred to the servant who was hired to take a child by the hand and lead them to school. Paul is saying that God's law was there to regulate people in order that they would be led to Christ. That's also why Paul said that Christ is the end (or the goal) of the law.

But for our own purposes here, we are simply noting that as adults we are all now away from our childhood regulators, our *pedagogos*, etc., and we are now *on our own*. If there is to be regulation in our lives it is now up to us, and not to anyone else. Yes, our church can try to put demands on us, and we need to be faithful to our vows to our church. However, the primary onus for regulation in our lives is ourselves.

That is why it is so important that we become creatures of habit. We must be creatures of self-regulation. Let's think of some of the things that should be involved in that.

STAY PHYSICALLY FIT

Whether we like it or not, we are bound to this earth only by the thin thread of our physical survival. There is no way for any of us to continue our earthly journey if our bodies disappear or are in one way or the other put out of commission. You can understand why James said that our life is like a vapor, appearing for a little while and then disappearing (James 4:14). We cannot be sure from one day to the next if we will be physically alive or dead. We have all known people who woke up strong and healthy in the morning and who were stone dead by evening. It is a sobering reality.

Having said that, however, we need to underscore the importance of good stewardship of our bodies. Our body is like a machine, though admittedly a highly complex one. God has created it in such a way that it requires maintenance. If I purchase a machine and never maintain it, I know that no matter how long it lasts it will not do as well or last as long as if I take pains to properly maintain it.

Maintaining my body means that I give it the proper input. What I eat is important. The regularity of my eating can also be important. If I eat things that weaken my physical constitution rather than strengthening it, I will eventually reap negative results.

In our modern and more sedentary societies, where many of us do not get proper physical exercise, it may be important for me to find a way to regularly exercise. Some of my readers do a lot of walking, which is an excellent form of exercise. However, some are like me and do relatively little walking. That is why at least three times a week I spend at least a vigorous half hour on a treadmill. It is my concession to the curse of modern over-sedentary living.

Perhaps it should be even more, though I believe that what I am doing is an important step toward staying fit physically. I do not do it for any reason other than to try to be a good steward of my physical body. I know when my physical body stops, I will be automatically *out of this world*.

The carcass I leave behind will have become useless. To be candid, I have no desire to make my exit from this world solely because I did not take care of the gift God gave to me when he gave me a physical body!

MAINTAIN MENTAL FITNESS

It is no less important that I stay fit mentally. A central part of maintaining good work habits is that I keep my brain active and productive. I want those billions of brain cells in my head to keep doing their job as long as possible! In fact, one of my prayers and hopes is that I will not live physically beyond the proper functioning of my brain. Who wants to spend time at the end of life in mental darkness?

The solution to this goal is for us to guard against mental laziness. Continue to be a regular and voracious *reader*. Guard against the temptation to passivity that can be fostered by watching too much television, spending too much time browsing through social media, etc. Continue to read good Christian biographies until the day you die! Read other excellent Christian books. Do not allow yourself to become mentally lazy!

TAKE MENTORING SERIOUSLY

If you have passed the age of 50 you should already have developed a life habit of deliberately mentoring younger ones around you. People can learn well and permanently from mature Christians who have won their respect. Part of being productive in the older years of your life means developing more deliberation in mentoring. If you have not done so, begin to ask yourself how you can pass on to the younger generation the values you have proven important in your own life.

The scriptures certainly encourage this principle of discipline. We see them most closely modeled by Jesus of Nazareth himself, who chose to spend virtually all of his productive ministry mentoring twelve disciples. The Apostle Paul also deliberately surrounded himself with a constantly modulating cadre of young men who were under his wings not just assisting him but learning from him.

Paul talked about the importance of older women teaching younger women as well, telling Titus: *"the older women likewise, that they be reverent in behavior, not slanderers, not given to much wine, teachers of good things—that they admonish the young women to love their husbands, to love their children, to be discreet, chaste, homemakers, good, obedient to their own husbands, that the word of God may not be blasphemed"* (Tit. 2:3-5). My prayer is that all of us will take more seriously the responsibility of mentoring others.

DON'T NEGLECT YOUR FAMILY

There two things that few men or women on their deathbeds have said: "I got too much education," or "I spent too much time with my family." My father used to facetiously talk about people he knew whom he described as "educated far beyond their ability to comprehend."

Maybe he was joking, but if he was serious then perhaps there have been at least a few people who have gotten too much education. Fewer yet, however, are those who have felt that they gave too much attention to their families. To the contrary, many of us need to make strong improvements in that area of our lives.

My primary point is that spending quality time with our families is important. Especially if I have children growing up in my home, they need my presence to guide them. Children should not grow up without the presence of a father in the home, unless it is totally impossible. They need to see modeled before them what godly manhood should be. I therefore must take time to pray with them, read the Bible to them, teach them the skills I can, and instruct them in the principles of life.

FORCE YOURSELF TO WRITE!

One thing that can do more than most people imagine to broaden the influence and leadership success of any minister of the gospel is to learn to be a good writer. Generally speaking, good writers will have an enormous advantage over others into the future. Moreover, good writing has a clear impact on our capabilities as speakers. It should therefore be of immense importance to all of us to know how to improve our writing skills. The answer to developing that advantage of our lives is fortunately quite simple: you learn to be a good writing by writing!

First, if you are a preacher, I urge you to start writing out your sermons, word-by-word. I know that will sound daunting to a lot of my readers, but please hear me out. Just do it, and then just keep at it. Whether you actually take your manuscript into the pulpit is not the most important issue. Some do, and some don't. Starting out as a young preacher, and continuing throughout his long pastoring career, my paternal grandfather wrote out all of his sermons, word for word. However, in his case he never took even a scrap of paper into the pulpit. Not even his Bible. Much of the reason there is that my grandfather, amazingly, knew the entire New Testament and most of the Old Testament by memory. My father has told me that as a child he would go into his father's bedroom on Saturday nights while his father lay flat on the bed quoting chapter after chapter from the Bible while my father followed him along with an open Bible. How I wish such a gift were hereditary! My grandfather likewise knew his sermon manuscripts, even though he had no notes in the pulpit with him.

In my own case, for at least the past ten years I have written out in full 95% of the sermons I deliver. I actually take the manuscript to the pulpit, but because I never deliver a sermon without have gone over it prayerfully and carefully many times (usually over at least a five-day period) I never have to slavishly read what is in front of me. Relatively few of my parishioners know that I actually have the entire manuscript in front of me.

Much of the reason is because in writing my sermons I have learned to write exactly the way I talk. Some people write as though they are trying to be "scholarly," which is not helpful and does not lead to good communication. As a result, they write far differently from their conversational English. Don't do that.

Maybe this sounds too difficult. Frankly, at least at first it is not easy, especially if you have not done it before. But I assure you that it is an investment in your future effectiveness that can be quite rewarding as you progress. Keep at it. Perhaps you can start by writing out one sermon a month. Then move up from there. In my own case, I would not think again any time in the future about not writing out what I am going to say.

However, I can almost hear someone thinking as they read this, doesn't this make it difficult or impossible for God to anoint the preaching? If I write it out ahead of time how can I expect the Holy Spirit to give me anointing as I preach? I nearly laugh when I hear that kind of response, because my own question is, why must we assume that the Holy Spirit cannot anoint writing every bit as much as he does the spoken word? I can tell you that when I write out my sermons, I end up very prayerfully going over and over what I am going to say, and I am convinced the Holy Spirit is right there with me, every step of that journey.

Writing out sermons is only one way to become a good writer, though for preachers it is a primary one. You can also develop the habit of writing down our thoughts as a part of our daily devotions. As you read the Bible and other excellent Christian writing have pen and paper at hand (or, in my case, be at your computer, where you can write things down without interrupting your devotional exercise).

Should you publish your writing? Maybe, and maybe not. Not everyone should publish. Not all pastors should publish. Beware of rushing into publication to early. My general advice is to be hesitant to publish, until you are sure you are ready, and that God is calling you to do it, and until you are convinced that you have a significant readership awaiting you. With a single exception, I did not publish books until I was past 60 years of age. By the time of the publication of this book I have put 25 books into print. In response to those who asked me about it before then, I would always say, "I am not ready yet. I need to get more experience." I am not saying that it is always ill-advised for younger men and women to publish. Some have done so with great success. But I dare say that much that has been written and published by pastors and leaders under 40 years of age would have been better left unwritten.

LEARN TO EFFECTIVELY USE SOCIAL MEDIA

Nowadays it is not possible to talk about the importance of writing without also mentioning social media. As each month progresses, we see more clearly that mastering social media for personal and ministry benefits is an important key to ministerial success. Social media can be both a blessing and a curse, however. As in every other aspect of our lives, finding good balance should be of high priority. There are people who waste many precious hours engaged in endless reading and chatting online when they should be monitoring things more closely and doing a much better job of stewarding their time.

Using social media judiciously to promote the gospel and to encourage uplifting communication within the Christian community is important. We have seen too many examples in the past of Satan trying to take over new means and methods of communication that have been shunned by God-fearing people. We should be very prepared to promote Christian blogging, preparing and broadcasting instructive webinars, and generally using every means possible to promote Christian values and the Christian message. May God give his children wisdom as they seek to stay abreast of the latest technology!

Oswald Chambers: A Man with a Great Work Ethic

A man who might never have become so widely known without the incessant work of his wife for decades after his untimely death at the age of forty-three is the Scottish Baptist, Oswald Chamber. He is best known for one of the most popular devotional books ever written, *My Utmost for His Highest*.

Even as a teenager, Chambers was noted for his deep spirituality, and he participated in the evangelization of poor occupants of local lodging houses. He was eventually trained for ministry at Dunoon College, a small theological training school near Glasgow, where he later assumed teaching responsibilities. He joined the Pentecostal League of Prayer, and thereby was led to friendship with Juji Nakada, a holiness evangelist from Japan. They later went together to God's Bible School, a holiness institution in Cincinnati, Ohio, where Chambers spent a semester as a teacher, and then on to Japan working with Charles Cowman, a co-founder of the Oriental Missionary Society.

Chamber's marriage to Gertrude Hobbs, in 1910, was highly fortuitous. His wife, whom he affectionately called "Biddy," was one of the most skilled stenographers of her time, capable of taking shorthand at 250 words per minute. Over the next seven-plus years of their marriage she took down and eventually transcribed hundreds of his lectures and sermons, most of which made it into book form in the decades after Chamber's death.

In 1915, a year after the outbreak of World War I, Chambers suspended the school he had started in London and was accepted as a YMCA chaplain. He was assigned to Zeitoun, Cairo, Egypt, where he ministered to Australian and New Zealand troops. Chambers raised the spiritual tone of a center intended by both the military and the YMCA to be simply an institution of social service providing wholesome alternatives to the brothels of Cairo.

When he told a group of fellow YMCA workers that he had decided to abandon concerts and movies for Bible classes, they predicted the exodus of soldiers from his facilities. "What the skeptics had not considered was Chamber's unusual personal appeal, his gift in speaking, and his genuine concern for the men." Soon his wooden-framed "hut" was packed with hundreds of soldiers listening attentively to his messages such as "What Is the Good of Prayer?" Confronted by a soldier who said, "I can't stand religious people," Chambers replied, "Neither can I."

Sadly, Chambers was stricken with appendicitis on October 17, 1917. A surgeon performed an emergency appendectomy, but Chambers died from a pulmonary hemorrhage. He was buried in Cairo with full military honors.

Several biographies of Oswald Chambers have been written. The best is by David McCasland, *Oswald Chambers: Abandoned to God*. As we read through the account of Chamber's life, we see a man who since early youth was highly disciplined in his work habits. He was almost always throughout his career faced with the challenge of wide travels, heavy administrative, as well as onerous teaching and preaching challenges. Yet Chambers worked as a selfless man, and at the same time maintained a strong private devotional and prayer life. During his final few months in Egypt, with heavy demands to minister to literally thousands of World War I soldiers, McCasland notes that "In the face of increasing demands on his time and energy, Chambers stringently maintained his early mornings alone with God. . . . Oswald's morning hour with God was the only undisturbed portion of his day.

Today we know Oswald Chambers primarily because of this faithfulness of his wife in putting his sermons and lectures into book form. His devotional, *My Utmost for His Highest*, has never been out of print. Yet when we look closely at his life, we discover that as a man he is worthy of very close emulation because he understood the absolute need for a sound work ethic. May God raise up more men like him in our own day!

INTEGRITY

I have already talked about integrity several times in this book. The reason is simple: integrity should be one of the most cherished qualities in our lives as believers and especially as leaders. Lack of adequate integrity is like a loose bolt on a huge girder holding up a building. No one may notice the loose bolt, and there may be no way it is apparently affecting the integrity of the building, but when pressures are increased the bolt can snap and lead to disastrous results.

There are many ways I could address this issue, but in this chapter let's think about the possibility of allowing little foxes to spoil the vine, and thereby compromise our Christian integrity. The context of that statement is in the Song of Songs 2:15, *"Catch us the foxes, the little foxes that spoil the vines, for our vines have tender grapes."* These foxes are obviously symbolic of something. We know from other Old Testament passages that foxes (or jackals, as they were also called) were considered as dangerous or destructive animals that could damage vineyards and cause the farmer to lose his investment and hard work.

You and I may or may not like foxes, but frankly foxes do not get good "press" in the Bible. You will recall that in the Old Testament Samson tied torches to 300 foxes and released them to destroy the grain fields of the Philistines. The foxes were the villains who did the dirty work. Later, that wicked man Tobiah taunted Nehemiah's rebuilding of the walls of Jerusalem by telling him, *"Whatever they build, if even a fox goes up on it, he will break down their stone wall"* (Neh. 4:3). In the New Testament, Jesus called Herod a "fox" as a way of rebuking his crafty and wicked nature (Luke 13:32).

In the passage in Solomon's song, the reference is to destructive things that are capable of spoiling the love of two people moving toward marriage. It is a reminder that we need to remove all potential threats that keep us from achieving what God wants us to achieve. Therefore, the bride specifically refers to the "little" foxes. What we are seeing is that it is often the little things—the things that some might overlook—that can spoil things of great value to us.

So, let's talk about some of those "little foxes" in our lives.

FIRST, **learn to be meticulously honest with truth**. The Bible is quite clear about the fact that lying is sinful. The Ninth Commandment says, *"You shall not bear false witness against your neighbor"* (Ex. 20:16). Leviticus 19:11 says even more to the point, *"You shall not steal, nor deal falsely, nor lie to one another"* (Lev. 19:11). In Revelation 21:8 *"all liars"* are included in the list of those who will face the eternal lake of fire. Any born again believer knows that the prohibition against lying is God's standard. To deviate from it lands me in trouble.

However, what about those "little white lies" in which I stretch the truth and end up saying something that is not spot-on true but something about six inches away? Is that okay? Are such "white lies" acceptable? Can they be excused, for example, when telling the truth might offend or hurt someone? Many people in our day would say so.

Let's think about it carefully. We should start by recognizing that the essence of lying is deceit. It is saying something (whether it is technically true or not) with the intent of deceiving my hearer. My motives may not be simply to deceive, but also perhaps to keep the peace, or to make myself look better than I really am.

Regrettably, we live in societies that often condition us to accept so-called white lies. One of my theology students told us in class that his church superintendent asked him to tell someone calling at the door that he was not around. It could have been okay for him to say he was "not available," but the message was to tell the visitor that he was "not around," which was obviously a lie. (Incidentally, my instinctive response to the student was to suggest to him that perhaps he should look for a different leader.) Or what about when we pad a resume with claims that are either exaggerated or simply not true? Our society often teaches us that when such things do not directly hurt anyone those "little" lies are acceptable.

What is wrong with this kind of thinking? Plenty. For one thing, there is no indication in the Bible that some sins are okay with God and others are not. God is still saying, *"The wages of sin is death."* It does not say, "Some sins are A-Okay, and others will lead you to death." Further, the acceptance of white lies is usually based on an idea that the end justifies the means. In other words, if I think something good might result from my little lie, then it is okay. Moreover, white lies are usually not orphans. They have a way of multiplying. One lie often calls for another, and then another, and eventually a whole string of lies follow.

What is the Bible solution? Paul got it right: *"speak the truth in love"* (Eph. 4:15). Telling the truth is not always easy, but Christians must *always* be known as truth-tellers, without any exceptions. God literally commands us to tell the truth, always (*"Therefore, putting away lying, "Let each one of you speak truth with his neighbor"* [Eph. 4:25]), because, after all, he is a God of truth.

SECOND, **watch your "thoughtsmanship."** I am borrowing that word from my father, who preached straightforwardly on this topic. I must be careful about what I allow myself to think. Proverbs 23:7 says, *"as [anyone] thinks in his heart, so is he."* Or, as you have perhaps heard before: "Sow a thought, reap an action; sow an action, reap a habit; sow a habit, reap a character; sow a character, reap a destiny." It all starts with our thinking, or our "thoughtsmanship."

Whether we realize it or not, our minds are active virtually 24 hours of every day, even when we are asleep. Our incredible brains never stop. Therefore, it is of extreme importance what is going through our minds. We must take responsibility for the fact that to a large degree God has given us the ability to control how we use our minds.

This is precisely why Paul told the Philippians, in a passage that should be taken to heart by all of us, *"Finally, brothers and sisters, whatever is true, whatever is noble, whatever is right, whatever is pure, whatever is lovely, whatever is admirable—if anything is excellent or praiseworthy—think about such things"* (Phil. 4:8). By the same token, it should be clear that there would be other things we should *not* think on: whatever is false, whatever is ignoble, whatever is wrong, whatever is impure, whatever is ugly, whatever is despicable, and whatever is neither excellent nor praiseworthy.

God has created us with natural curiosity, and with a desire and thirst for knowledge. Yet God is not pleased for us to needlessly expand our knowledge of evil. Unless you have a specific reason to learn more about particular evils (such as a law enforcement officer understanding how certain types of crime are carried out), turn your mind away! You should never feel embarrassed to not be well informed about all the details of the evil going on in the society around you. Keep a pure mind. Learn instead to be a purveyor of good news. Let your mind be soaked in scripture.

Paul told the Romans that we need to be transformed by the renewing of our minds. Our focused, informed and trained minds are a great key to our Christian success. He also reminded the Corinthians that the reason they could not discern spiritual truth was because of immature minds (1 Cor. 2:14). Don't forget also that the concept of repentance in the Greek language is a "change of mind." When we come to Christ worldly, ungodly, wicked and dirty thinking is washed away and is replaced by a changed mind. Hallelujah!

God wants us to be as proactive as possible in replacing the "stinking thinking" of the world with the truth of God. The best way to source that is in the pages of the Bible. Being transformed by the renewing of our minds happens as we soak ourselves on a day-by-day basis in the Holy Bible. We do it in our personal devotions, our family Bible time, our weekly Bible studies, etc. We need to be a part of a Bible-believing, Bible-reading, Bible-preaching, Bible-soaking, Bible-singing and Bible-loving church.

These things do not happen by accident. There is no magic formula that will suddenly change our thinking and renew our minds. Rather, day-by-day we must renew our determination to fill our minds with God's truth and to throw overboard every thought that is contrary to God. Paul challenged the Corinthians, *"For the weapons of our warfare are not [a]carnal but mighty in God for pulling down strongholds, casting down arguments and every high thing that exalts itself against the knowledge of God, <u>bringing every thought into captivity to the obedience of Christ</u>"* (2 Cor. 10:4-5). That is true "thoughtsmanship" in action!

THIRD, **be honest with money issues.** I do not believe there is likely any one of us who has not given in at some point to the temptation to be less than totally honest with money issues. However, I also believe that learning the discipline of steadfast and totally trustworthy honesty with our money is essential for Christian maturity and victory. Mature believers are unflinchingly honest when it comes to their money. They have learned to leave no room for misrepresentation or dishonesty. They can be unflinchingly trusted. They have also learned that the love of money can be a root of all kinds of evil, and they are therefore on their constant guard against carelessness and the temptations of Satan.

There are many ways to be dishonest with our money. It can be as simple as the temptation to put someone off who is appealing for financial help. We may be tempted to say, "I have no money," when in reality we know we have money, but we do not believe we should respond to that particular appeal. It can include accepting to make a purchase for someone and not giving an accurate report after the expenditure. It can include not being factual in our report to the government when paying our taxes. In fundraising, it can involve misinforming potential donors about the nature of the need at hand.

Honesty should be at the core of our character traits. Integrity with money should be high on our list of values. I have personally learned a long time ago that I am not good at keeping financial records, so I never accept such responsibilities for anyone except myself.

As an organizational man, I always need to be surrounded by people who are far more capable than I in handling money. It is also one of the reasons why I have never gotten near the church money during my pastoring days, right up to the time of this writing. Other responsible and accountable people must handle the money, and I must never touch it. That is the good and proper policy for *all* pastors.

If you have a tendency toward weakness in this area, I urge you to take steps to bring correction into the matter. That may mean completely changing some of your procedures. It could also mean deliberately setting up an accountability relationship where you seek advice from a close friend to help you be strong in this area. Do not let this "little fox" spoil your vine!

FOURTH, **do not entertain evil surmising.** Here is another little fox who has spoiled a lot of Christian vines. Nearly every day we find ourselves surrounded by people who love to gossip and who pass along all kinds of speculation about the evils supposedly being done by others. Conspiracy theories are hatched by the boatloads, and eagerly passed on to people who cannot understand all that is happening around them and who are quick to pick up any sinister ideas about who is behind it all. My advice to you as a leader is to *learn how to stop your ears* to about 99.9% of it!

The Bible takes a dim view of people who love to gossip and pass along their evil surmising. Proverbs 11:12-13 says, *"He who is devoid of wisdom despises his neighbor, but a man of understanding holds his peace. A talebearer reveals secrets, but he who is of a faithful spirit conceals a matter."* Or what about the reminder in Proverbs 16:28 – *"A perverse man sows strife, and a whisperer separates the best of friends"?*

Paul describes the sinfulness and lawlessness of people who have turned their backs on God, in Romans 1. He says that God turns them over to their sinful natures, including to things such as *"deceit, evil-mindedness; they are whisperers, backbiters,"* and then he notes that *"those who practice such things are deserving of death, not only do the same but also approve of those who practice them"* (Rom. 1:29-32).

Especially when our church or the society around us is going through trying times there will always be an uptick in the swirling of rumors and surmising. There will always be people peddling the latest conspiracy theories about who is behind all of the negative things that are happening. In those circumstances it is highly important that we have strong leaders who can help people to get their eyes off of the surmising and onto Jesus and onto the word of God. Learn to focus on the things that are eternal! Teach yourself and others around you to turn a deaf ear to the conspiracy stories.

I had a pastor friend many years ago who over the years gained a sordid reputation as a church splitter. He has long since gone to his eternal reward. But his reputation during his lifetime was that every time he pastored a church, as one controversy or the other arose, instead of being the much-needed peacemaker he always managed to take sides and stir the pot until finally the church was divided and split asunder. Please do not be that kind of pastor!

Approach this little fox of evil surmising with wisdom. Finish him off with a heavy dose of Christian love, sound Bible teaching, and turning everyone's eyes toward Jesus. You can do it.

FIFTH, **be cautious about your relationships with the opposite sex.** It is a common saying among ministers of the gospel that there are three principal areas of temptation that can conspire to undo a holy man of God: money, sex and fame. Everyone understands the nature of those three things, though they are usually given different names, such as money, women and pride; or girls, gold and glory; or females, funds and fame.

My personal problem with these common listings of the three areas of temptation is that I believe the second area should not be labeled as "women," or "girls" or "females." Let's be clear on this: the problem we are talking about there is not really women, but rather the *uncontrolled lust* of men. God created women to be sexually attractive to me. It was his idea. But he also set boundaries and going over those boundaries is primarily because we men do not control our lust. James says, *"Each one is tempted when he is drawn away by his own desires and enticed"* (James 1:14).

What I am saying is that God created women as beautiful, virtuous and holy. A godly woman is priceless, and it is not *she* who is the problem here, but rather the out-of-control sexuality of men. Let's be honest about these things. Yes, I know that quite occasionally there are women who literally sexually prey on godly men, but I will also tell you that (1) the kind of "godly" men they go after, usually, are those who have already begun to give in to pride and self-glory and who are therefore easy prey, and (2) men of deep godliness are extremely unlikely to ever fall for such women. King David went after Bathsheba because he allowed himself to gaze at something that was forbidden, until his will crumbled.

Are you sure about how you would respond if (God forbid) an ungodly woman suddenly tried to throw herself at you? I definitely know how I would respond. Why? Because I have rehearsed it in my mind. It's like a security officer who has been trained about how to handle an emergency. If he has good training, he will act virtually instinctively to do the right thing when the unexpected emergency is thrust open him. That's why I have already decided what I would do if a woman who is not my wife suddenly and deliberately tried to seduce me. It would be "game over" in about three seconds. Finish. How about you?

❖ I am talking about being cautious in my relationship with the opposite sex. There are a number of little foxes here that can push us in the wrong direction. That is why my personal etiquette that has become part of my fixed habits includes, among other things.

- ❖ I never counsel a woman alone, but only with the presence of my wife or another man (such as a fellow minister).

- ❖ I do not give a woman a ride in my car unless there is someone else in the car as well.

❖ I keep my hands off of all women except my wife, unless under rare circumstances to gently lay my hand on her head (in the presence of others) when praying for her.

❖ I do not discuss matters of sexual intimacy with women, except discreetly in a counseling situation in which my wife is the principal counselor.

❖ If I sense that a woman may be nursing an inappropriate relationship toward me, I take steps to withdraw and hand her over to others, without wasting time.

Why are these things necessary? Because I fear those little foxes that can spoil the vine, and this is definitely an area in our lives where those things can begin to happen.

SIXTH, **learn to avoid tribalism like the plague.** Over the past few years many of us here in Nigeria have understood a bit more what it means to avoid something *like the plague.* First, we faced the Ebola crisis in 2009. Then in 2020 we spent weary weeks and months running away from the coronavirus plague. We found ourselves doing all sorts of things the government told us would help us to *avoid the plague.* Thankfully, the plague never raged as we were at first told it might.

There is another plague I am talking about here, and that is the plague of tribalism. It is a little fox that is always ready to spoil our vine if we will allow it. Tribalism is wicked. It is a part of our fallen sinful nature. It is the idea that one ethnic group is superior to another.

The social dynamics of tribalism are identical to racism. Racism is the idea that one race is superior to another. White/black racism is an issue that has been especially a part of our national experience in the USA, where I grew up. We fought a bloody Civil War over it from 1860–1865 that took over 700,000 lives. The reason was that America was founded on the belief that "all men are created equal," yet black men and women had been excluded. As a result of the war, all slaves were freed.

Regrettably, however, with the assassination of President Abraham Lincoln immediately after the close of the war, things began to go backwards again, with the racist Andrew Johnson and the Democratic party in the lead. For 100 years, even though slavery had been abolished, blacks were persecuted and disenfranchised in about every way possible. Incredible atrocities were committed against them, including hateful public lynching. Only over the past fifty-plus year, with the passing of the Civil Rights Act of 1964, have things begun to be corrected. There is still a long way to go, though I thank God for the serious progress that has been made.

Regrettably, there is no parallel of that kind of purposeful dismantling of tribalism in Nigeria. Slavery was finally outlawed in Nigeria, though not until more than fifty years after the USA took their own step in that direction. Yet a bloody Civil War was fought here over tribal issues, from 1967–1970. Many people believe that the primary conflicts in Nigeria are Muslims vs. Christians, yet serious research has shown that at least 80% of so-called religious conflicts in Nigeria are in actuality not about religion but about ethnic hatred and killing.

I only mention all of this because I believe it is highly important that every one of us living in Nigeria (and anywhere else in Africa, for that matter) should be on the red alert against any and all forms of tribalism. I must nurture and maintain a deep conviction that I am not by creation any better than other human beings. Everything I have is a gift from God, for which I must be grateful. My tribe or my race is not in any way superior.

Paul said it quite succinctly – *"He* [God] *has made from one blood every nation of men to dwell on all the face of the earth"* (Acts 17:26). He further expressed his conviction about Christian equality extending to every other social denominator:

> For you are all sons of God through faith in Christ Jesus. For as many of you as were baptized into Christ have put on Christ. There is neither Jew nor Greek, there is neither slave nor free, there is neither male nor female; for you are all one in Christ Jesus. And if you *are* Christ's, then you are Abraham's seed, and heirs according to the promise. (Gal. 3:26-29)

I believe the Christian Church is the best possible arena in our society to display the Christian standard of equality between all races and ethnicities. We must seek to be thoroughly de-tribalized people, through and through. We must fight against tribalism wherever it sticks up its ugly head, whether in our families, our churches, our communities, or in our country. We must continually learn to treat all of our brothers and sisters with equality. That is the best testimony we can give our world that has yet to know the great love of Jesus.

Billy Graham: Man of Integrity

In 2018, at the age of 99, Billy Graham went home to be with the Lord. He was one of the great spiritual giants of our generation, loved and admired by men and women of virtually all walks of life and all branches of the Christian Church. Billy Graham was known primarily as an evangelist. It is estimated that during his lifetime he spoke to live audiences, radio audiences and television broadcasts to more than 2.2 billion people. One special television broadcast in 1996 alone may have received a viewership of as many as 2.5 billion people worldwide. As a result of his crusades, Graham preached the gospel to more people than anyone in history. What a remarkable life![21]

One of the primary reasons for the success of Billy Graham was that right from the start of his ministry he adopted ministry patterns and personal habits of high integrity. He was a man who was known and trusted for his personal honesty and transparency. Those who worked with him

---

[21]https://en.wikipedia.org/wiki/Billy_Graham. Accessed 11 June 2020.

constantly attested to his open heart and mind and that it was clear that Graham practiced what he preached.

Billy Graham was careful with the handling of money. After his ministry began to attract thousands, then tens of thousands and eventually millions, money flowed in. Yet Graham refused both to handle the money himself or to amass personal profit, as others might have. He was totally transparent in money matters. Not only that, but early on he drew around himself a large board of mature men, all of whom were much his seniors in age. He asked them to serve as his directors and advisors. People knew they could trust the Billy Graham Evangelistic Association because of their transparency and the obvious truth that it was not there as a vehicle of personal wealth for one man. Graham was practicing strong personal accountability all along the way.

Graham also drew up his own list of personal rules for relating to women other than his wife. The nature of his work demanded that he be away from his wife and family for weeks and sometimes months at a stretch. Wherever he went women were eager to talk with him, get counsel from him, and otherwise express their appreciation for his ministry. Yet Billy Graham drew up rules quite similar to the ones I have mentioned above. In fact, my own rules were at least in part inspired by the earlier example of Billy Graham. It included never being alone with a woman who was not his wife, etc.

Finally, I should note that Billy Graham blazed new trails in many Christian circles by demanding that all racial barriers be removed in his crusades and other meetings. Though some were opposed to his insistence on total equality between races and bringing together blacks and whites with an equal welcome at his meetings, Billy Graham was unflinching in his stand for equality. His example did much to change the attitudes of multitudes of others. One man of sterling integrity had proven to all of us that leading by example could make a huge difference. Thank God for the long and productive life of this wonderful servant of God!

ACCOUNTABILITY

One of the earliest Christian movements in search of New Testament holiness was monasticism. It is regrettable that quite early in Christian history the goal of personal holiness that was clearly laid down in the New Testament was misunderstood and then turned into works righteousness. Unfortunately, it was the same mistake made by the Jewish people in Old Testament times. Paul pointed out in Romans 9 that the failure of the Jewish people in receiving the salvation God offered to them during Old Testament times was that they did not seek it by faith, but rather as though it were *"by the works of the law"* (Rom. 9:32).

In like manner, the early Christians, after the close of the New Testament era, largely lost sight of the pursuit of godliness or holiness by faith and began a long line of efforts to pursue it by their own works. They had forgotten the simple teaching of Galatians 2:8-9 (that we are *"saved through faith"*) and Acts 26:18 (that we are also *"sanctified by faith"*).

One of the efforts toward the attainment of holiness that arose starting in the Third Century was monasticism. It has been rightly noted that monasticism is the longest and most sustained effort in Christian history toward the attainment of holiness. There remain today many hundreds of Christian monasteries all over the world, some of them dating back more than 1,000 years. St. Anthony (251-356 AD) is regarded as the father or patron saint of the movement. For periods of many years Anthony remained holed up alone in a cave in the Egyptian desert. Today monasteries often separate men from women, often demanding total personal poverty, and monitoring lives of strict religious practices and self-denial.

We may have a certain admiration for people with such discipline and self-abnegation. However, we must also recognize that God did not create us as people who ideally should live alone, separated from other human beings. Monastic life is not normal or ideal human life. Holiness is not something to be lived out in solitude. Neither on earth nor in heaven did God ever intend for it to be so. In his preface to "Hymns and Sacred Poems" published in 1739, John Wesley warned against the idea that holiness should be pursued in any kind of isolation. He wrote, "Solitary religion is not to be found there. 'Holy solitaries' is a phrase no more consistent with the gospel than holy adulterers. The gospel of Christ knows of no religion but social; no holiness but social holiness."[22]

---

[22]https://urbanabbeyoldmarket.blogspot.com/2016/07/no-holiness-but-social-holiness.html. Accessed 23 June 2020.

Certainly one of the principal benefits of social life is the opportunity for accountability. We live our lives before God, but we also live them before others. Responsible accountability should be experienced in both of those arenas. The Bible tells us plainly that we are accountable to God. *"For we must all appear before the judgment seat of Christ, that each one may receive the things done in the body, according to what he has done, whether good or bad"* (2 Cor. 5:10). Jesus was even more specific: *"But I say to you that for every idle word men may speak, they will give account of it in the day of judgment. For by your words you will be justified, and by your words you will be condemned"* (Matt. 12:36-37).

It is also important that within the body of Christ we learn the benefits of accountability to our fellow believers. I am convinced that those who are leaders in the Church have even greater needs for accountability. A pastor should be consciously and transparently accountable to his congregation. Among other things that means his life must be an open book to others in such a way that he has a wholesome report and wholesome reputation with all of his flock. He must be their primary model of transparency, honesty, integrity, truthfulness and discipline in such a way as to not bring disrepute on the gospel. In short, we are accountable not only to God, but also to those who surround us. Paul expressed that obligation of leaders to the Corinthians, saying, *"We give no offense in anything, that our ministry may not be blamed"* (2 Cor. 6:3).

It is regrettable that the "big man" syndrome has become so entrenched in some sectors of the Nigerian Church that it is assumed that the leader is above criticism. As a result he becomes untouchable. He is not held to account for his moral conduct. Accountability is basically absent. This does not bode well for the health of any congregation.

We see the power of accountability demonstrated within scripture. In Acts 2:42-47 we are given a window into the life of the Early Church, immediately after the Day of Pentecost. What we see there is that the church was a tightly woven body in which there was sound teaching and preaching, social and spiritual interaction, eating together, praying together, and strong care and concern for every single member. There was no concept of anyone so far about the others that they were excluded from accountability.

Later on, in Galatians 6:1-2, Paul addressed the issue of the effective application of accountability. He knew that in any context of accountability there would be instances in which faults and failure would be highlighted and brother and sisters who had erred would need to be called to order. That is how accountability works. So, Paul said, *"Brethren, if a man is overtaken in any trespass, you who are spiritual restore such a one in a spirit of gentleness, considering yourself lest you also be tempted. Bear one another's burdens, and so fulfill the law of Christ"* (Gal. 6:1-2). Paul's understanding was that the highest percentage of needed correction within the body of Christ would come automatically where there was effective accountability and genuine love and humility.

As leaders we have primary responsibilities to keep ourselves unspotted from the world and to lead by example. That is why Paul urged Timothy, *"Watch your life and doctrine closely. Persevere in them, because if you do, you will save both yourself and your hearers"* (1 Tim. 4:16). Eugene Peterson's *The Message* renders it like this: *"Keep a firm grasp on your character and your teaching. Don't be diverted. Just keep at it. Both you and those who hear you will experience salvation."*

I believe accountability for ministers of the gospel must be on at least three levels. This is what I have practiced across the years.

FIRST, I must be accountable in clear and transparent ways to my church. If I am pastoring within a denomination that means close accountability with my superintendent, bishop or overseer. I must live with an awareness that transparency before my church leaders is paramount. If I have pastoral responsibilities over a congregation it further means that I must have an accountability relationship with them as well. If I am to be a godly leader meriting the respect of my followers, my life must be an open book to my deacons, presbyters or other congregational leaders. I must live before them in undisguised transparency. I must let them know clearly that I am not above criticism or accountability as their leader.

I must be willing to be vulnerable before my congregation by being candid with them in appropriate measures about my own weaknesses. I must not be unwilling to help those around me learn from some of my own past failures, where it can be shared in a constructive context.

SECOND, if I am a married man, I must have appropriate accountability with my wife. Wives who give strong reports about the integrity of their minister husbands are wives who are sharing in an effective accountability relationship with their husbands. Any husband who lives with ongoing personal secrets that he is not willing to share with his wife is courting disaster and does not merit full respect. Much more so is this true with a spiritual leader of a church. This is one of the primary reasons that for many years I have had a filter on my computer and other devices that are capable of accessing the internet (e.g., iPad, smart phone). That filter blocks objectionable sites and also sends a bi-weekly report directly to my wife. She knows where I go on the internet. The bottom line is that I should never visit any internet site that I would be embarrassed to share with Jesus or with my wife!

THIRD, I must develop deliberate peer accountability relationships. This is normally an especially difficult step for pastors and other church leaders. It is only accomplished as a result of resolute determination. The reason it is difficult is that pastoral ministry and church leadership tend to be lonely occupations. People are constantly opening up to their pastor, but pastors usually have no one to whom they themselves are equally open. They find it difficult to find anyone with whom they can exercise effective accountability.

Over the years I have had numerous one-on-one accountability relationships with peers in ministry. It has never been easy to sustain those relationships, but they have been of inestimable importance to me. Usually those relationships have involved regularity, meaning that either on a weekly or bi-weekly basis we agree to meet together.

Face-to-face meetings are ideal, but I have also had effective long-distance relationships, including international ones.

A typical peer accountability session involves candid sharing of a short list of areas where each person feels a need for correction, improvement or a brotherly check-up. It is a time for sharing advice, and for prayer together. A typical accountability session does not have to be lengthy. Much can be accomplished in a 15-minute session if both persons are determined to take it seriously. In short, peer accountability is extremely important for those of us in ministry!

The Early Methodist Class Meetings

The moment I think about accountability my mind turns to John Wesley and what he taught his own followers about accountability. First, however, was his experience with the Holy Club, at Oxford University, established in 1729, during his student days. Second was his instituting of the Methodist Class Meetings, very early on in his ministry, after his evangelical conversion of 1738.

The Holy Club was an informal gathering of Oxford students, the most notable members of whom were John and Charles Wesley and their younger colleague, George Whitefield. All three were to eventually become famous as driving forces behind the great Evangelical Awakening that shook the entirety of the United Kingdom and stretched across the Atlantic to America.

Part of the purpose of the Holy Club was a serious drive for accountability. Among other things, it involved each member asking themselves every day in their private devotions twenty-two questions. They would in turn seek ways to hold one another accountable on those questions. I believe it is worthwhile to contemplate exactly what they were asking themselves:

1. Am I consciously or unconsciously creating the impression that I am better than I really am? In other words, am I a hypocrite?

2. Am I honest in all my acts and words, or do I exaggerate?

3. Do I confidentially pass on to another what was told to me in confidence?

4. Can I be trusted?

5. Am I a slave to dress, friends, work, or habits?

6. Am I self-conscious, self-pitying, or self-justifying?

7. Did the Bible live in me today?

8. Do I give it time to speak to me every day?

9. Am I enjoying prayer?

10. When did I last speak to someone else about my faith?

11. Do I pray about the money I spend?

12. Do I get to bed on time and get up on time?

13. Do I disobey God in anything?

14. Do I insist upon doing something about which my conscience is uneasy?

15. Am I defeated in any part of my life?

16. Am I jealous, impure, critical, irritable, touchy, or distrustful?

17. How do I spend my spare time?

18. Am I proud?

19. Do I thank God that I am not as other people, especially as the Pharisees who despised the publican?

20. Is there anyone whom I fear, dislike, disown, criticize, hold a resentment toward or disregard? If so, what am I doing about it?

21. Do I grumble or complain constantly?

22. Is Christ real to me?

I am sure the kind of discipline instilled in one another through the Holy Club had at least something to do with the fact that these men went on to become true spiritual giants. Interestingly, we know that neither John nor Charles Wesley at the time of the institution of the Holy Club had a clear knowledge about the New Birth. However, they were both earnest seekers after God. Thankfully, by 1738 they both came to a clear knowledge of salvation and were launched into fifty years of incredible ministry.

Near the beginning of that ministry, toward the end of 1739, eight or ten persons who appeared to be deeply convinced of sin came to John Wesley, in London, earnestly seeking salvation. They asked him to spend some time with them in prayer and advise them how to flee from the wrath to come, which they saw continually hanging over their heads. Soon a few others joined in the same appeal.

Wesley saw this as a God-sent opportunity. He set a day for them to come together, on a weekly basis, every Thursday evening. The number of those interested quickly expanded. Wesley began to give them advices from time to time, always concluding their meetings with prayer suited directly to their needs.

This was the rise of what was called the United Society, first in Europe, and eventually also in America. These societies were described as "a company of men having the form and seeking the power of godliness, united in order to pray together, to receive the word of exhortation, and to watch over one another in love, that they may help each other to work out their salvation."

It was the beginning of small group accountability for which the Methodist movement was long known. As the number of participants grew in each society, they were eventually divided into smaller companies, called classes, in order to have a more effective accountability of every single member of the group. The ideal number of participants in the classes was about twelve persons, out of which one person was chosen as the leader.

The responsibility of the class leader was to see each person in his class once a week at least, in order (in the words of the original instructions):

(1) to inquire how their souls prosper;

(2) to advise, reprove, comfort or exhort, as occasion may require;

(3) to receive what they are willing to give toward the relief of the

preachers, church, and poor.

It was further required of the leader to meet the minister and the stewards of the society once a week, in order:

(1) to inform the minister of any that are sick, or of any that walk disorderly and will not be reproved;

(2) to pay to the stewards what they have received of their several   classes in the week preceding.

There were many reasons why Methodism became the leading church in America within less than fifty years after it was established there, but certainly one of them is that they understood and put into practice the discipline of accountability. We can learn from them ourselves, even today in faraway Nigeria!

SIMPLICITY AND FRUGALITY

Simplicity and frugality are not listed among the historic Seven Cardinal Virtues, but if I had my own way they would be. They are two closely related virtues that I hope I will always cherish. I cherish being a simple and frugal man. I commend these virtues to all of my students and mentees.

For one thing, I believe simplicity is a virtue with great power to draw us closer to God and to make us more like Christ. Jesus of Nazareth was a man of simplicity. There was nothing opaque or hidden about him as a human being, though the mystery of his deity was unfathomable by all around him. He spoke truth in simple words, without even a slight hint of hypocrisy, arrogance or ostentation.

Jesus found it natural to praise little children and those who were of pure heart. That is where he saw the tranquility of simplicity. Young children are by nature simple and untroubled, and so, too, are Christian saints who are focused wholly on God. Yet for all too many of us our lives are much more complicated than they should be, and as a result our prayers and our devotions are also complicated.

Simplicity starts in our hearts, and not our heads. Some of us worry far too much about being correct and not enough about having warm hearts. It would do us all good to learn to pray to God for simplicity, and to understand that we are not necessarily as wise or as correct as we might think we are.

Over the years I have told my students repeatedly things like, "I reserve the right to be wrong," and "When I get to heaven I will spend the first few years just laughing at myself, and wondering, 'How did I ever have such crazy ideas down there!'" When I say those things, what I am trying to tell them is that I want to always have a humble attitude about my own ability to get everything right. I want to be simple enough to be a continual and life-long learner. I do not ever want to outlive my ability to acknowledge that I was wrong.

Many times, I have told my bewildered theology students, "I know that my theology is wrong." Frankly, while it is a true statement, what I am trying to do is to jar them awake to realize we are all on a learning journey. Learning is co-terminus with living. When we stop learning we stop living. Therefore, the reason I know my theology is wrong is that even though I do have strong convictions about many of my theological positions I also know I am constantly learning and therefore constantly making little corrections here and there to my previous thinking.

Because I am still alive with an active brain, I know that process is not over. Ergo, of necessity, I know that at least *some* of the cherished theology I am now carrying around in my head is wrong. Happy is the man or woman who can maintain that kind of attitude!

ARENAS OF SIMPLICITY

Simplicity should be a way of life for us. Simple and unassuming people are pleasant to be around. They do not put up unnecessary barriers that make others feel uncomfortable, as if they cannot rise to their high standard of expectation. Those who are transparent and simple are the ones who do not feel threatening to others they encounter on life's journey. This simplicity is displayed in a variety of arenas.

All of us should desire to be people of **simple speech**. For those of us who are preachers that would also obviously include our preaching. When we speak, we should never use words or expressions designed to impress our listeners with our presumed intelligence.

That reminds me of the story of two old men who were sitting on the front row at church because they were so hard of hearing. After the preacher got up to speak and had been going for a good ten minutes one of the old men leaned over to the other one and asked in a loud voice that could be heard by others around them. "What is he talking about?" His friend turned to him and replied, "He hasn't said yet." Apparently his speech was not very simple.

Let us be adequately simple in our speech. Let our words be sound and edifying. Paul had several things to say to Titus about soundness in doctrine, for example, in Titus 1:9-13. Then in the next chapter he said, *"Likewise, exhort the young men to be sober-minded, in all things showing yourself to be a pattern of good works; in doctrine showing integrity, reverence, incorruptibility, sound speech that cannot be condemned, that one who is an opponent may be ashamed, having nothing evil to say of you"* (Titus 2:6-8). Simplicity of speech is important!

I believe that same simplicity should be carried over into our writing. We must learn to **write with simplicity**. I do not mean with bad grammar or syntax or needlessly butchering the English language. There is no virtue in that, of course. Rather, I mean writing with my audience in mind so that I do not talk over their heads and befuddle them with my language. I know some brilliant writers who have important things to say, but who write with such complicated language that it is difficult and tiresome to follow them. After struggling a few pages, I want to go take a nap, because they have tired me out. I am tempted sometimes to think that they might even be trying to impress me with their intelligence. (I think I already reminded us earlier that my father once told me about a man whom he described as "educated far beyond his ability to comprehend"!)

This is also why I urged you in an earlier chapter to force yourself to write out your sermons. Write them in the simple language of a good pastor or preacher who is trying his best to speak words that his audience understands. Let us be simple in our writing!

We should also be **simple in our relationships**. All of us at one time or the other have had opportunity to meet and possibly even get close to men or women of high reputation. If so, we may have observed that some of them are difficult to communicate with. We tend to feel uncomfortable in their presence because we never know what they are thinking and do not know exactly how to conduct ourselves with such "important" people. By contrast, you may also have met some great men or women who are quite easy to talk with. They have the capacity to put us at ease in their presence. The reason is usually that they have learned to be simple in their relationships. That is what we should all strive toward.

The spirit of genuine humility involves principles such as Paul describes in Romans 12:10, *"Be kindly affectionate to one another with brotherly love, in honor giving preference to one another."* Or think about Jesus' advice in Luke 14:7-10, *"When you are invited by anyone to a wedding feast, do not sit down in the best place, lest one more honorable than you be invited by him; and he who invited you and him come and say to you, 'Give place to this man,' and then you begin with shame to take the lowest place. But when you are invited, go and sit down in the lowest place, so that when he who invited you comes he may say to you, 'Friend, go up higher.'"* That is simplicity in our relationships.

Simplicity also includes our **dress and demeanor**. It is both unwise and wasteful to overspend financial resources on clothing that is primarily worn to draw attention to ourselves. Dressing well, as our budget allows, is a good habit, especially for those in Christian ministry. Yet there should be a quiet dignity about our clothing and demeanor. However, it is simply wrong for us to wear clothing that is designed primarily to draw undue attention to ourselves. Dressing in flamboyant outfits should be left to high society movie stars and others whose values do not reflect the teachings of the Bible.

As I will mention more below, simplicity should also extend to my attitude and practices toward **material goods**. You may remember the story of a man who came to Jesus begging him to intervene with his brother who did not want to share the inheritance with him. In Jesus' response he said, *"Take heed and beware of covetousness, for one's life does not consist in the abundance of the things he possesses'"* (Luke 12:15). Having material goods is not a Bible standard for success. Accumulating more and more things as a measure of our value or stature is not a God-honoring goal. In fact, Jesus strictly warned against what he called *"laying up treasure on earth"* (Matt. 6:19-23). Let us learn how to be simple in our attitude and practices about material goods.

THE WISDOM OF FRUGALITY

Frugality is the virtue of avoiding waste and excess. I am sure this message is far more urgently needed in America where I grew up than here in Nigeria. In America it is all too easy to go into deep personal debt in pursuit of nonessential luxuries. Self-discipline is becoming harder with each succeeding generation. But it is good for us also here in Nigeria to learn the virtue of self-denial and to refuse to give in to the temptations brought on by modern advertising.

Benjamin Franklin, one of the founding fathers of America, and whom I may call a folk philosopher, once said, "If a man wishes to remain economically and emotionally independent, frugality is an essential virtue to develop. Think what you do when you run in debt; you give to another power over your liberty." It is a known fact that Franklin and other American founding father feared that too much luxury makes a nation weak. They would often point to the ultimate failures of the Greeks and Romans as examples of what happens to a nation when it lets prosperity go unchecked by temperance and frugality.

Nigeria is far from the poorest country in Africa. There are millions in this country who have food, clothing and shelter and much more on top of that, which is how the scriptures define those who are *rich*. Paul says in 1 Timothy 6:8-9, *"having food and clothing, with these we shall be content. But those who desire to be rich fall into temptation and a snare."* By implication he is defining riches as having food, shelter and clothing and *other things in excess above that.* The word "clothing" that Paul uses is literally translated "coverings," which include both clothing and shelter. Paul also believed that with riches come enormous dangers. The message of the Bible is that it is not sinful to be rich, but that it is exceedingly dangerous.

What I am saying is that sooner or later many of us will have hard choices to make about frugality. When we reach the point that we can at last afford finer clothing, richer dining, and more elaborate transportation, entertainment and luxuries what will be the financial principles that will guide our lives? Many of us, despite living in a country as economically depressed as Nigeria, have not made a determination to continue frugality as a life principle no matter our economic prosperity.

American founding father John Adams often preached against what he labeled "effeminate luxuries." Though he was a wealthy man, Benjamin Franklin lived a simple life. He made efforts to eat and dress plainly. Today, unfortunately, the vast majority of Americans who revere the memory of Franklin and others of his generation have nevertheless lost sight of the importance of frugality. For the current generation of men and women who have grown up in a period of unprecedented affluence, living frugally seems to many of them downright silly and old fashioned. Yet I remain persuaded that if anyone wishes to be economically and emotionally independent, as well as spiritual strong and alert, frugality is an essential virtue to develop.

I believe one of the essential foundations for a proper life of simplicity and frugality is a Spirit-directed depth of consecration accompanying an experience of deeper sanctification. I can testify that in my own life that is what made the total difference. I have shared this story before, but please be patient as I mention it again.

As a young man of eighteen years of age, after walking with the Lord in triumph and joy for several months, in the earliest days of my conversion, God brought me up short with the realization that I did not have a pure heart. I had assumed that I was filled with the fulness of the Holy Spirit and that I did not have any need of a further work of cleansing or empowerment in my life.

To my greatest shock, I discovered over a process of several days and weeks, however, that I was still harboring an unChristlike spirit within me. I was walking in full obedience to God, but I began to discover strong elements of fleshly, ego-centered anger. I discovered an impure spirit of jealousy that no one else could possibly have seen, in which I went so far as to wish that my dearest friend and brother were dead so that I could receive some of the praise others were heaping on him instead of on me.

Most of all I saw a spirit of ugly pride, in which I secretly imagined I was the most spiritual young man around, and that I could likely do a better job of pastoring our church than my much older and more mature pastor. In short, I was in trouble and I eventually realized that I was headed to certain doom if I did not find a way to get rid of my load of inward sin.

It was after spending long days getting to the bottom of my unclean heart and praying it all out to God and renouncing it and pleading to God for a mighty operation of the Holy Spirit to cleanse me and fill me with the fulness of the Holy Spirit that God took me to a place of deep consecration I had never known before. It was truly my Gethsemane, so to speak. There is was, in the most private encounter I had ever had with God, that he probed my heart to the very bottom and asked me some of the toughest and most unwelcome questions I had ever heart in my life.

Interestingly, the very first question God asked me had to do with this very question of simplicity and frugality. Yet the way God asked me about it was a simple question: "Would you be willing to serve me the rest of your life and never have money?" It was an incredibly tough question to answer. It was as real as though God himself had shown up in physical form to probe me. It was not theoretical.

God was asking me if I would be willing to serve him the rest of my days and never have any kind of steady or sufficient income. The question was so absolutely real that in my mind and heart I could almost feel the hunger pangs. It was the kind of question that no one would like to hear, yet I realized that it was real and that saying "no" to God was virtually unthinkable. The only way I could avoid the question would be to walk out of the room and say goodbye to the Holy Spirit. I knew I could not do that.

I thank God that he enabled me to say a definite "yes" to that question. I can testify that it is because of that question that all across the more than fifty succeeding years I have *never* asked the question about how much money is involved when I have made a change of employment. I have worked at times for zero salary, and at other times I have been well paid. Most of the time I have lived on far less financial income than other missionaries around me. Yet by the grace of God I have practiced for more than fifty years giving away more than one-half of what comes into my hands. I have learned to be frugal. I own no property anywhere in the world. I do not own an automobile. My heart is free.

John Wesley's Simplicity

If there ever was a church leader who could have lived in great ease and even luxury it was John Wesley, especially in his latter years. Wesley lived to a ripe old age, dying peacefully at close to 88 years. It is rightfully said that there may never have been another man in history who spent as many hours on the back of a horse, traveling enough miles in that manner to circumvent the entire globe ten times. I have enjoyed the novelty of horseback riding a good number of times in my own day, but I have had enough of it to say "NO THANKS" as a regular mode of travel. I still have memories of the soreness of my poor legs after particularly long rides.

But Wesley's toughness did not end there. He was a man who deliberately denied himself of many simple pleasures that he was well able to afford financially. Over the years John Wesley became enormously successful as an author and book seller. He wanted his people to read, and he did everything in his power to make that possible. He widely distributed his own writings, including his journal, his collected sermons, his popular *Primitive Physic* (a book of medical cures, which went through more than 100 editions), *Explanatory Notes on the New Testament, A*

Compendium of Natural Philosophy, etc. He also abridged classical writings and made them available at low prices so his people could be more broadly educated. The sale of his books often gave him the equivalent of over N5,000,000 a year in today's currency, which was enough in the Eighteenth Century to make him wealthy in nearly anyone's estimation.

It is said that one year his income was £30, so he lived on £28 and gave away £2. The next year he received £60 so he lived on £28 and gave away £32. The third year he earned £90 and once more he lived on £28 and gave away £62. In other words, he just kept what he needed to live on without falling into debt and gave away the remainder. At one point he left off eating of meat and reverted to potatoes, to save expense. Simple food and inexpensive clothing became his life-long practice. He once boldly state, "If I leave behind me ten pounds, you and all mankind bear witness against me that I lived and died a thief and robber." True to his word, when Wesley died, he had barely more than half that amount to his name.[23]

At the foundation of Wesley's secret to simplicity and frugality was his famous dictum about money: "Gain all you can; save all you can; give all you can." First, by "gain all you can" Wesley meant that conscientious Christian character demands that we work diligently at our livelihood. He firmly believed Christians have obligation to be as economically fruitful as possible in their chosen

---

[23]David Malcom Bennett, *John Wesley: The man, his mission and his message* (Capalaba: Rhiza Press, 2015), Kindle loc 1492-1490.

field. Without endangering life or health, without indulging in business lacking Christian integrity and honesty, and without harming one's mind or neighbor, the Christian is admonished to gain as much as possible by honest industry. Wesley said:

> Use all possible diligence in your calling. Lose not time. . . . If you understand your particular calling, as you ought, you will have no time that hangs on your hands. . . . You should be continually learning, from the experience of others, or from your own experience, reacting and reflection, to do everything you have to do better to-day than you did yesterday.[24]

Second, Wesley said *"save all you can."* His meaning was simple: we are not to willingly waste anything, not even a sheet of paper or a cup of water. "I do not lay out anything," he said, "not a shilling, unless as a sacrifice to God."

He explained that saving all one can has nothing to do with putting money into the bank. Wesley believed money is far better immediately invested in God's kingdom than being put into a bank. He said: "A man cannot properly be said to save anything, if he only lays it up. You may as well throw your money into the sea, or bury it in the earth." Wesley went so far as to profess that he would rather throw his money into the sea than put it in the Bank of England.

There are three specific admonitions that fall under Wesley's injunction to *save all you can*. For one thing, he

---

[24]Wesley, *Works*, VI, 130.

stressed forcefully the importance of saving money by wasting absolutely nothing on gratification of the flesh.

> Do not waste (anything) . . . particularly, in enlarging the pleasure of tasting. I do not mean, avoid gluttony and drunkenness only: an honest heathen would condemn these. But there is a regular, reputable kind of sensuality, an elegant Epicureanism, which does not immediately disorder the stomach, nor (sensibly at least) impair the understanding; and yet (to mention no other effects of it now) it cannot be maintained without considerable expense. Cut off all this expense! Despise delicacy and vanity, and be content with what plain nature requires.[25]

Wesley was even more insistent that Methodists save all they could by avoiding superfluous and expensive apparel and fancy adorning of their houses. He believed that to wear expensive clothing and particularly to be in the height of fashion, when less expensive clothing could be had, was a crime against those poor who might otherwise be benefited by the money laid out. Besides, to gratify desire for superfluous apparel and adorning of houses only served to heighten those desires. He noted, "When you lay out money to please your eyes, you give so much for an increase of curiosity — for a stronger attachment to these pleasures which perish in the using."

Save all you can, Wesley urged, by not needlessly throwing away your money on your children. On the one hand,

---

[25]Wesley, *Op cit*, VI, 131.

don't waste your money and ruin them by providing delicate food, gay or costly apparel or any other superfluities. On the other hand, do not waste money by leaving it to your children to throw away after your death. Normally one should give his money out himself for the glory of God, and only in extreme cases where children fully understand the value and use of money could Wesley countenance the idea of parents leaving money to their children.

Wesley gave his followers practical tests to discern scriptural soundness of expenditures. When in doubt, he suggested they ask four simple questions: 1) Am I thus acting as a steward of my Lord's goods, and not as proprietor? 2) Am I doing this in obedience to his Word? 3) Can I offer this expense as a sacrifice to God through Jesus Christ? 4) Have I reason to believe I will receive a reward at the resurrection of the just for this expense? He suggested the following prayer to accompany any financial outlay:

> Lord, thou seest I am going to expend this sum on that food, apparel, furniture. And they knowest, I act therein with a single eye, as a steward of thy goods expending this portion of them thus; in pursuance of the design thou hadst in entrusting me with them. Thou knowest I do this in obedience to the word as thou commandest, and because thou commandest it. Let this, I beseech thee, be an holy sacrifice, acceptable through Jesus Christ! And give me a witness in myself, that for this labor of love I shall

have a recompense when thou rewardest every man according to his works.[26]

In the third part of his dictum, Wesley urged his followers to *give all they could*. He ties this strongly to the concept of stewardship. We are stewards of God's possessions, not proprietors over our own wealth.

Wesley believed God's plan of giving for the faithful is four-fold. It explains the context in which he believed all giving should take place. First, we must provide things that we need: food, clothing, what is moderately required for preservation of the body in reasonable health. Second, we must provide those things also for our spouse, our children and others in our household. Third, if there is surplus, we must make provision for others who are part of the household of faith. Fourth, if there is still surplus, as we have opportunity, we must do good unto all others within our sphere of life.

Wesley recognized that only by giving all he possibly could would he be effectually secured from laying up treasure on earth. Writing to his followers he said directly:

> Do you give all you can? You who receive five hundred pounds a year, and spend only two hundred, do you give three hundred back to God? If not, you certainly rob God of the three hundred.[27]

---

[26]Wesley, *Op cit,* VI, 134.
[27]Wesley, *Op cit,* VII, 362.

May God give us wisdom in our own day to be people of simplicity and frugality. It we can achieve that virtue I am convinced it will go a long way to providing an important witness to our own generation.

LIFE-LONG STUDENT

One thing I like about the apostle Paul is that he fervently desired and expected to end his life in the saddle. In other words, he wanted death to interrupt his work. He wanted to remain productive for God until he drew his last breath. That is also my own desire. It is clear that none of us has ultimate control of our future, and as believers we continue to accept the will of God no matter what circumstances that might entail. At the same time, I doubt if any of us in his or her right mind would want to outlive our ability to be of use to others, even if at a reduced level of action. I will write more about that in my final chapter.

Closely related is what I am writing about now, which is the goal of being a life-long student and continuing to learn right down to the end. In one of his less-than-stellar moments Solomon wrote, *"Of making many books there is no end, and much study is wearisome to the flesh"* (Eccl. 12:12). To understand the book of Ecclesiastes it is important to remember that it was written toward the end of Solomon's 40-year reign. Especially since he had to try to manage living with 700 wives and 300 concubines, I am sure he was by then a very tired old man. It seems as we listen to him that he was pretty much fed up with earthly life in general. His perspective in Ecclesiastes is helpful. His book is a reminder to all of us of the futility of putting our hope and values too highly in *anything* that terminates with this life.

However, let me talk to those of us who have only one wife or one husband, which I assume is virtually all of my readers. First, we can thank God that we have moved beyond the era of polygamy and are now taking our spouses seriously as co-laborers or yokefellows in God's vineyard. Second, we can agree that one of the secrets of remaining productive until we draw our last breath is to continue to value learning as much as possible all the way to the end.

John Fletcher was one of the godliest men of his day. He was John Wesley's designated successor, though Wesley eventually outlived him. Fletcher once said, "An over-eager attention to the doctrines of the Holy Spirit made me in some degree overlook the medium by which the Spirit works, I mean the word of truth, which is the wood by which that heavenly fire warms us. I rather expected lightning, than a steady fire by means of fuel."[28] What Fletcher was saying was that our lives (both spiritual and intellectual) consist primarily in the steady, ongoing of adding "fuel" to our spiritual and mental fire. Therefore,

---

[28]Quoted in Samuel L. Brengle, *Helps to Holiness*, 16; *Take Time to be Holy*, loc 1487; John Fletcher, *The Works of the Reverend John Fletcher* (London: John Mason, 1859), 166.

unless my fire has gone out completely, I need to keep adding fuel as long as I am alive.

For one thing, as long as I alive and am able, I can promise my readers that I will continue to read excellent Christian biographies. I have done that most of the days of my Christian life. Some of them I have read and re-read numerous times, and I am constantly looking for new ones. I will also continue to read excellent devotional works. I will seek to expand my knowledge by keeping abreast of scholarship in the fields where I am most engaged. Why? Because I believe that learning and living are co-terminus. When I stop learning, I stop living.

I can further say for all of us that prayer and meditation in the Word of God will keep the sanctified believer full of power, love, and faith. In short, full of God. On the contrary, failure to pursue these basics of learning and nurture will result in spiritual and mental weakness and dryness. As long as I live, I hope to be able to give a ready answer when anyone asks me, "What have you been reading lately?"

MAINTAINING A SHARP INTELLECT

One of the important steps to ensure that we are life-long learners is to maintain a sharp intellect. Our brain is the control center of our body. As we age there is a natural tendency for our brain to respond more slowly. If we do not do anything to check that process, we can eventually become totally sluggish in our minds. Our learning processes will grind to slow pace or a complete halt. However, there are a number of positive things we can and must do if we are to remain positive, active and productive right down to the end.

FIRST, regular bodily exercise is highly important. The key is regularity. Some say that it should be daily, but in my own case I am careful to exercise vigorously not less than three times weekly (nowadays on Tuesdays, Thursdays and Saturdays). Good physical exercise can include anything from vigorous walking, to running, lifting weights, etc. Good physical exercise benefits us not only physically, but also mentally. It helps ward off depression and builds up our all-important immune system. There are reliable studies that show that good physical fitness increases our mental sharpness as we grow older.

SECOND, eating a balanced and proper diet is important. As much as possible our eating times should be with regularity. I am not a medical doctor, but I can assure you that any good doctor would be willing to give you sound advice about what to avoid and what to include in a healthy diet. Eating fruits, vegetables and whole grains is important, as well as antioxidants. Avoiding excessive carbohydrates and frankly excess of any food is important.

THIRD, getting enough sleep and sleeping on a regular timetable is important. I know when many of us were younger we sometimes ate and slept at all kinds of odd hours, but as we age it becomes more and more important that we sleep adequately and regularly. A mind that is well rested is able to perform at its best. If you are not getting adequate sleep at night you may also consider taking a nap in the middle of the day.

John Wesley is an example of a man with highly regulated sleep habits, even though he spent much of his time on the road. No matter where he was, unless he had accepted to join an all-night prayer meeting, he would go to bed promptly by 10:00 pm and would rise at 4:00 am. He also had the gift of being able to lie down in the middle of the day and almost instantly fall asleep for a short nap, waking up 15 or 30 minutes later much refreshed.

FOURTH, take active steps to see that you continue to learn. Learn to think of yourself as a life-long student. If you have access to a reasonable library, make use of it. Usually a library is also a great and quiet place to relax and focus on study. Don't overlook opportunities to enroll in special classes for adults that are usually available in any town of reasonable size. Also, make a habit of reading new books at least once a month. For many years I have used a Kindle, similar to an iPad, and on it every single day I am reading from several books. My mind is constantly reaching out for more knowledge.

FIFTH, find ways to exercise your mental muscles, not just your physical muscles. Working on puzzles or other mental teasers is a great idea. We know that older people who do crossword puzzles do better on cognitive skills that those who do not. Although computer games can become virtually addictive and great timewasters, they can also help in maintaining mental agility, as is also true with many other types of board or card games.

Focus On Theodore Roosevelt

There have been many great men and women down through the ages who have exhibited a commitment to life-long learning. One of them that quickly comes to my mind is Theodore Roosevelt, the 26th president of the US who served from 1901 to 1909, as the youngest man ever elected to that office, at 42 years of age. In national polls, Roosevelt is usually ranked among the top five most popular US presidents.

After he left office, Roosevelt became the first US president to visit Africa. He was a statesman, a conservationist and was the author of over forty books. He was quite sickly as a child, but deliberately overcame his handicap by committing himself to a life of vigorous masculinity, as a celebrated soldier, hunter, explorer, and naturalist. He exercised regularly and took up boxing, tennis, hiking, rowing, polo, and horseback riding.

"Teddy" Roosevelt (the fifth cousin of the later 32nd president of the US, Franklin D. Roosevelt) was a man with multiple claims to fame. He excelled as a war hero in the Spanish-American War, as the Assistant Secretary of the US Navy, as Governor of New York, as the Vice President of the USA, and eventually as President.

There are innumerable demonstrations that Theodore Roosevelt was committed to life-long learning. Throughout his life he was an avid reader, reading tens of thousands of books, at a rate of several per day, in multiple languages, making him probably America's most well-read president. He was also an avid reader of poetry. He edited the *Outlook* magazine, and in all wrote some 40 books, including his autobiography, *The Rough Riders*, and his two-volume *History of the Naval War of 1812*, which is still in print today. The account of his 1909–1910 African expedition is entitled *African Game Trails*.

It is doubtful that any of my readers or I myself can match the reading and writing legacy left by Roosevelt. Each of us has his or her own level of talent and intelligence. But certainly, every one of us can commit to a similar life of commitment to perpetual and life-long learning. May God enable us not only to achieve that, but to do it wholly for his own honor and glory!

FAMILY FOCUS

Across the centuries there have been great Christian heroes who for one reason or other have chosen to not marry. The Apostle Paul is an example from the Bible. He apparently felt that his missionary duties did not create an acceptable environment in which he could settle down and do justice to the duties of a husband and father. Francis Asbury, the father of American Methodism, is another example, and for similar reasons. In our own day, John R. W. Stott, the long-time pastor of All Souls Church in London and a great friend of Africa, was a Christian minister who lived into his 90s and never married.

As much as we might admire these men, most of us do not want to emulate them when it comes to marriage and families. We cherish the fact that we are either married or that we plan to marry at God's appointed time and in his will. That is what prompts me to lift out this crucial secret to ministerial success: an exemplary family focus.

We live in an age in which more than ever our world needs excellent models of Christian family living. No one can deny that there are huge forces in the world seeking to tear apart the nuclear family. Single-parent homes especially in some of our western societies, are multiplying at an alarming rate. Something needs to be done to stop worrisome trends of fathers abandoning mothers and children growing up without the benefit of the nurture of both a mother and a father.

The most important thing that we can do in this situation is doubtlessly our own personal example. If we hope to succeed in Christian ministry let us start by making an unbreakable determination to be the best husband or wife possible, and then become as faithful, loving and guiding a parent as God can make us.

Marriage is the initiation and the core of a strong family. It is impossible to have a strong family without a strong marriage. Some of us came either from polygamous homes where the modeling of Christian marriage was not possible or from homes in which our fathers abandoned us while we were growing up. If so, that makes it doubly important that we determine to throw off the bad examples with which we were raised and to establish a Christian marriage that is both scriptural and also exemplary for those to whom we will minister. Having a strong marriage cannot be overvalued in that regard.

There are many ways in which marriage is viewed all around us. Some view marriage with what I may call a *functional* model. They see it as two people coming together and revolving the relationship around a division of labor. They are not primarily focused on true companionship or oneness of spirit, but simply on a sort of business partnership, in which everything is viewed from the standpoint of cooperation in function. Often, when this is the model the marriage goes on with a minimum of true love, and little regard for the emotional and spiritual needs on both sides.

A second marriage model could be labeled the *companionship* model. In this one, there is more of a focus on equality and sharing. It is obviously an improvement on the functional model, though it is still not Bible-centered. Here there is a greater attempt for husbands and wives to value one another, and a greater liberty in sharing their lives together. Yet it still falls short of the scriptural pattern.

One of the great passages of scripture which I believe gives us a pattern for proper biblical marriage is Philippians 2:2-7. That passage obviously has a broad range of applications, but at its core it is a call for all of us to be Christlike. With reference to what I am talking about in this chapter, it provides at least four keys for what I would call the *oneness* model in marriage. God designs that in Christian marriage the husband and wife become one, where neither person dominates with the commanding attitude many of us might have seen from our own parents.

This oneness model provides what I believe are the two greatest needs within a marriage: significance and security. Generally speaking, the greatest felt need of husbands is significance. They need to hear words of affirmation. A man's primary focus is usually on his work, or career, and receiving from his wife words of affirmation or commendation concerning his work is crucial to his emotional stability.

On the other hand, the greatest felt need of wives is usually security. They need to know that they are safe. That safety is not only physical, but also emotional and economic. The primary focus of wives is usually on their family. They need to know that their husband is providing the necessary security for the family to grow in strength, peace and adequate prosperity.

The keys to which I referred in Philippians 2:2-7 are important. A strong oneness model marriage needs all four of them. First, it is important that both husband and wife be *of the same mind* (*"fulfill my joy by being like-minded"* . . . *"of one mind"* [v.2]). It takes time and effort for a married couple to become and remain like-minded. There will always be times of disagreement and even sharp clashes, unless the wife has been so cowered down that she dares not speak up (may God forbid!). If a married couple ever tells you that they never have a quarrel or disagreement, you should know immediately that one of them is probably living in timid subjection! Strong marriages involve strong efforts to be of one mind.

Second, the oneness model requires that husbands and wives maintain the same love (*"having the same love"* [v. 2]). Love in marriage is not just an emotion, though our emotions are important. Marital love is primarily a fixed and irrevocable decision, or determination.

Third, husband and wives must be united in spirit. The spirit of a oneness marriage is constantly seeking for the unity of the marriage and the betterment of our partner. Paul describes it as *"in lowliness of mind let each esteem others better than himself"* (v. 3). When that happens, there is a unity of spirit that cannot be obtained in any other way.

The final key is what Paul describes in verse 6 and 7, where we see a clear focus on God's purpose. Just as Jesus *"made Himself of no reputation, taking the form of a bondservant, and coming in the likeness of men,"* so we in our marriages see and understand that God had a purpose in bringing us together as man and wife. Once we see that purpose, clearly and unselfishly, there is no power that can break our unity and our final success.

After more than fifty years of marriage, I can now look back on some of the things I believe helped me and my dear wife to sustain victory in our oneness relationship. We certainly made a huge number of mistakes, and there are lots of things over those years which we both wish we had done differently, yet we have a huge number of things for which to praise God. Let me share some of our own secrets:

<u>Learn to celebrate the things you have in common</u>. All marriages bring together people with differences. If our spouses were mirror copies of ourselves both of us would likely suffer. We need the differences, even when they sometimes bring disagreement and require great and sometimes uncomfortable or even painful compromises.

In our own case there are a great number of things Emma Lou and I have in common. We frequently celebrate them.

❖ We are both fixated on a primary devotion to God, and we both know that as much as we love each other our love for God is primary.

❖ We both love frugality and simplicity. We came from large families with meager resources, and we hardly spend money on ourselves. In fact, we vie with each other on whom we can help.

❖ When our children were at home, both of us believed in strong child discipline. We took seriously not sparing the rod, and teaching our children self-discipline, and the results are evident today in their adult lives and that of their own children.

❖ We both have always had a strong commitment to cross-cultural missions, even before we began our own long career in that area.

❖ We both take seriously caring for widows and orphans.

❖ We have had a common mind for many decades focusing on the training of African leadership.

Frankly, if we wanted to do so we could focus and fuss and worry about all the things we do not share in common, but that is not our desire. I love to travel and see new places, and Emma Lou loves to stay home (unless there is a grandchild out there somewhere). We have chosen to not obsess over our differences but celebrate what we have in common.

<u>Learn to speak one another's love languages</u>. In 1992 Gary Chapman published a book that has gained a lot of attention in marriage seminars: *The Five Love Languages*. In the book Chapman says that there are primarily five ways in which husbands and wives give and receive love. He further stresses that it is highly important that husbands and wives study themselves and understand their own personalities in order to more effectively communicate love to each other. Chapman is correct. Emma Lou and I have made serious attempts to discover each other's love language(s), and it has been of great help to us.

The five languages Chapman talks about are: (1) words of affirmation, (2) giving and receiving of gifts, (3) quality time, (4) deeds of service, and (5) physical affection. Emma Lou and I have discovered over the years that the giving and receiving of gifts is *not* our primary love language, for either one of us. That does not mean that we attach zero value to gifts, but it is just not high on our list. All of the others are important to us. Emma Lou highly values quality time. She feels a lot of love from me when she knows that I have deliberately set aside time and other responsibilities so that I can focus on her exclusively. She also highly values physical affection. When I take time to embrace her and hold her, she responds quickly.

On the other hand, she knows that my primary love language is words of affirmation. Perhaps it is in part because while I was growing up my parents were quite stingy with their words of affirmation. When I did very well at something, they were reluctant to praise me or commend me, perhaps out of fear that I would get a "big head." As a result, when Emma Lou commends me for a job well done it means very much to me.

I challenge every one of my readers to look carefully at the love language of your spouse. I have a friend who gives lots of gifts to his wife and child. However, he has not understood that those gifts do not mean much to them. What they really want is for him to take more time for them and to show more physical affection. Don't make that kind of mistake. Study your spouse. Learn to speak the love language that is most meaningful to him or her!

<u>Don't hide things from each other</u>. A marriage that is full of secrets being held between husbands and wives is not a stable marriage. I am not talking about little petty secrets, but the withholding of significant information and tending toward deceitfulness toward each other. In marriage we should learn to be as open with each other as possible.

Openness in marriage must be established over a process of time. My wife and I have had a permanently fixed habit of never going anywhere without letting each other know where we are going. Unless I am in a far country where I cannot give her the details of my daily movements, she knows at all times where I am and where she can find me, and vice versa.

In a similar vein, we do not keep significant financial secrets from each other, except in small areas, and even there we are always willing to be open with each other. The only exception we have about the revealing of secrets is when it comes to pastoral counseling. We are both into counseling as a part of our ministry. Yet we both know that what is divulged to us in confidence in counseling sessions is not something we ever share with each other, unless the counselees have given us clear permission to do so.

<u>Worship together on a daily basis</u>. This is the bedrock of a solid oneness marriage. There is no stage in our marriages where family worship is not highly important. When our children were young it was important. When they were growing into teenage years it was important. When they left home, it was important for the two of us to continue. Every single day we read the scriptures together and pray, and often we sing together as well. We fill our minds with the word of God before we go to bed at night. This is one of those non-negotiables in our marriage. Thus it should be with every other Christian marriage as well.

<u>Learn to listen</u>. Marriage brings an inevitable constant need for understanding and compromise. In order to accomplish that we must learn to learn to each other carefully. Understandings and conflicts will arise yet learning to listen to each other will go a long way toward peace, love and unity. I am convinced that my wife should be my best friend. Generally speaking, we should be able to share more freely with each other than with any other person.

RAISING GOD-FEARING CHILDREN

I cannot leave this topic of family focus without saying something about the task of raising God-fearing children. My observation is that there are not an adequate number of professed Christian fathers and mothers who have this as the primary goal in their task of raising children. However, so far as my wife and I are concerned this is absolutely Number One for us. It has always been so.

Today I can testify with deep gratitude to God that all four of our children, who are now themselves moving into middle age, are fervently serving God as Christian leaders in their respective environments. They all have significant commitments to ministry within their churches, though only two of our four children and four children-in-law are ordained ministers. What is much more important, however, is that every one of them has a vibrant testimony of a strong relationship with God. They are truly God-fearing people.

I do not believe these things happen by accident. Rather, they come as a result of following scriptural principles and scriptural patterns, and those things start from even before the hour of their birth. Let me mention a short list of some of the things I believe are of great importance in achieving this kind of goal. I cannot be exhaustive, and indeed this is fodder for a much longer "epistle" at some point.

First, to raise God-fearing children you must **begin early and never quit**. Raising children for God means that even before they are born you and your spouse are praying over the unborn child and committing him or her to God and praying God's blessing on them. Then from birth onward that child must hear the sound of prayer and the reading of the scriptures every single day of their life. They must know that more than any other thing you could ever wish for in their lives number one is that they would know God and serve him throughout life.

Second, you must absolutely **lead by example**, and not just by precept. Your children will learn soon enough that you are not perfect, and frankly that is not what they are looking for. They will soon see your heart, and if you yourself are a genuinely God-fearing person you will be able to show them what godliness and holiness looks like. They will learn to pray and desire to pray if they see you earnestly praying. They will learn to cherish the meeting together of God's people if they see that you cherish it yourself. They will become generous people if you show them your own generous heart.

Third, part of this also means that you will **model humility before them**. I believe all of my children can probably remember times when I have gotten down on my knees in front of them (so I could meet them eye-to-eye) and have said something like, "Daddy was wrong. Will you please forgive me?" You must let them know that your value of a God-fearing life includes your willingness to be totally honest about your mistakes, your failures and your sins.

Fourth, if you are to raise God-fearing children you must **teach them the scriptures**. Teaching the scriptures starts even before children can read, and yes, even before they can talk. The reading of the Bible, the memorizing of scripture, and the reading of age-appropriate Bible stories is extremely important. Our oldest daughter quoted the entire 23rd psalm just prior to her second birthday. I am sure she had little or no idea of what "green pastures" or "enemies" meant at that time. Yet today, when she is now past fifty years of age, her heart, mind and soul are constantly filled with scriptures which she is generously lavishing on her children and others on a daily basis.

Fifth, it is of great importance that you **engage them in ministry**. There is nothing more powerful in the shaping of a God-fearing child than to place them in situations where they themselves minister to others. Start it at a young age. When we were newly arrived in Nigeria it only took our twelve-year-old second daughter a few weeks to start a neighborhood children's Bible club without our initiation or at first even without our knowledge. On weekends we took all of our children to visit churches where they, too, joined us on the platform to sing special sons, including our three- and five-year-old boys. Frankly, it somehow got into their blood. They loved it then, and they still love it today.

Sixth, it is important for us to **expose our children to others who love God**. Steering our children toward friendships and close associations with other God-fearing people is important. Peer pressures are crucial among children and young people, which makes it doubly important that they are brought into close friendship with people who share our own Christian values. As our children we are growing up and engaging more and more in Sunday school and youth service ministry, we took pains to make sure that they were mentored by older youth whom we could see were of a godly nature and who clearly knew Jesus. In that process there was a reinforcement of their tendency to love the things of God.

Closely tied to this, I believe, is the importance of teaching our children to enjoy themselves and have fun in constructive ways that are consistent with Christian character. Certainly, we can all remember great times of family fun and enjoyment, yet it was never far away from our focus on living God-fearing lives.

Finally, we should let our children know that **God values all kinds of work and every honorable career**. I was very careful as my children were growing up to let them know that I did not have a career choice for them, and that God needs good men and women in every imaginable honorable career. There is something natural about a father wanting to see at least one of his children pursue his own occupation, yet that was never my objective. Today God has blessed me and my wife with four children, each pursuing four very different lines of work.

William and Catherine Booth

One of the great families in modern times that exemplified strong Christian values was the family of William and Catherine Booth, founders of the Salvation Army. "General" William Booth was born in 1829 and lived into his 80s. He and his wife Catherine founded the Salvation Army in 1865, as the East London Christian Mission, reaching out to the dregs of English society with both temporal and spiritual help. While many today think of the Salvation Army only as a social organization, William Booth and his followers were focused squarely on evangelism and holiness.

William and Catherine Booth worked hand in hand not just as husband and wife but as co-ministers in the Christian harvest. Catherine's powerful addresses to sometimes very large crowds were nearly as cherished as those of her "blood-and-fire" evangelist husband. Booth's early motivations for the Salvation Army were both to preach a no-holds-barred message of repentance and salvation, but also to convert poor Londoners such as prostitutes, gamblers and alcoholics to Christianity, giving them what was referred to as the three 'S's': soup, soap, and salvation.

One of the most remarkable things about William and Catherine Booth was their family. God gave them eight children, between 1856 and 1868. All eight lived to adulthood, which was relatively rare during the Victorian era in England. They were blessed with five girls and three boys. Even more rare, however, was the fact that all eight children became productive and highly successful officers (ordained ministers) in the Salvation Army. Only one child, Marie, who suffered an accident as a child and lived a largely invalid life, was unable to serve with the same energies of her siblings, even though she played a service role as best she could.

Their oldest child, a son, Bramwell, took his father's place as "General," upon his father's death in 1912. Twenty-some years later, William and Catherine's seventh child, Evangeline, became the fourth "General," and the first female to lead the movement. By then the Salvation Army had spread virtually around the world with the message of salvation, holiness and succor for those in need.

The success of this Christian family eventually touched millions of lives. Much of it had to do with a mother and a father who instilled Christian values, the Bible, and a love for ministry into the hearts of all their children. May God raise up more such people in our own day!

GROWING OLDER WITH GRACE

I assume most of my readers are not using a walking stick, or even thinking about it. Great! Maybe this chapter looks a little boring to you. However, hear me out, because sooner or later you will ask someone to find you that walking stick and thank them for their efforts. The question I want to raise in this final chapter is how you and I can grow older not haphazardly or awkwardly, but with grace.

My thinking along these lines was stirred up several years ago after listening to a sermon by Pastor Tom Nelson, of the Denton Bible Church in Texas. At least the broad outline of what I want to share with you I owe to Tom, from his series of sermons on 2 Timothy. Tom is one of the best preachers I have listened to, even though we do not agree on some of the finer points of theology. My consolation is that we will both get ourselves straightened out theologically when we get to heaven and will likely discover that we were both wrong.

Many of us have been a bit baffled by the book of Ecclesiastes, written by King Solomon probably in the final months of his forty-year reign. It is an essay on the true meaning of life, in which he shows us the dark side of what it looks like when one seeks for meaning and contentment apart from God. If God is taken away from our understanding our lives are just a meaningless cycle with no ultimate purpose and no satisfaction. *"Vanity of vanities"* (Eccl. 1:2), he cries out, and reminds us that at the end of life there is a sense in which what happens to all the animals happens to us as well. Our bodies came from the dust of the earth, and sooner or later *"the dust will return to the earth as it was"* (Eccl. 12:7). The only redeeming hope, he reminds us, is that *"the spirit will return to God who gave it."*

Psalm 90 is also a part of the Wisdom Literature of the Old Testament, like Ecclesiastes. In that psalm, which in the superscription is described as a "prayer of Moses," we see similar reasoning as we hear from Solomon. *"The days of our lives are seventy years; and if by reason of strength they are eighty years, yet their boast is only labor and sorrow; for it is soon cut off, and we fly away"* (Ps. 90:10). Therefore, we are given an important reminder: *"So teach us to number our days, that we may gain a heart of wisdom"* (Ps. 90:12). The understanding is that we must make every day count. They are not numberless. Whether we like it or not, we are all on a count-down to our final day on Planet Earth. The days will not go on forever. Therefore, let every day be used wisely.

Second Timothy is Paul's last writing that we know about. In it he acknowledges that his race is finished. He seems to know he is in his final imprisonment, in Rome. His travels are over. We all know those ringing words: *"I have fought the good fight, I have finished the race, I have kept the faith"* (2 Tim. 4:7). Look at those words in context:

> *For I am already being poured out as a drink offering, and the time of my departure is at hand. I have fought the good fight, I have finished the race, I have kept the faith. Finally, there is laid up for me the crown of righteousness, which the Lord, the righteous Judge, will give to me on that Day, and not to me only but also to all who have loved His appearing."* 2 Timothy 4:6-8

What follows in the rest of this 2 Timothy 4 chapter is one of the most personal and poignant passages in all of Paul's writing. The personal emotions Paul pours into this passage are amazing. These are his closing words to what had been a dramatic life, especially starting with his conversion to Jesus on the road to Damascus well over thirty years earlier. What we see is a man of incredible persistence and tenacity, who has faced the unthinkable time and time again but who is a decided victor, through and through.

Not, by the way, that everyone in his day would have agreed with him. Paul was not everybody's hero. We should not forget that to many people Paul was not a victor but a defeated man. They saw him as a failure. He was rejected by the vast majority of his Jewish brothers and sisters. They regarded him as a virtual traitor to what they believed. He was also rejected by the Greek philosophers of the day, as we can see in Acts 17. They scoffed at his idea of revering a resurrected Jesus. In addition, he was rejected by a number of heretical Christians who taught that new Christian believers had to cling to their own Jewish customs in order even to be authentic Christians.

To all of those people Paul was not a victor but a problem and a failure. To top it all off don't forget where Paul was. He was in a stinking hole in the ground in the infamous Mamertine prison in Rome, literally awaiting his execution. That is why in verse 13 he pleads to Timothy, *"Please bring my cloak."* He was shivering in a cold, dank cell. It is also why in verse 21 he says, *"Make sure you get here before winter."*

But is Paul discouraged? Not in the least! Look at verse 8 again:

> *Finally, there is laid up for me the crown of righteousness, which the Lord, the righteous Judge, will give to me on that Day, and not to me only but also to all who have loved His appearing.*

Hallelujah! Paul is filled with great hope. He has every confidence that there is something in store for him that he is going to momentarily lay hold of.

I think the question we need to ask ourselves as we read these words is whether we, too, like Paul, are true Christian finishers. How possible is it for us to speak this way? Look at it closely. In verse 6, we can see the importance of having a clear perspective of *who we are*:

For I am already being poured out like a drink offering, and the time for my departure is near.

That is significant imagery. Paul sees himself as a libation, as someone poured out by God for the sake of his own generation. He is saying that God is in total control; not Paul himself. He is a sacrifice being offered by God for the benefit of others. Wow! Here is a man totally in the hands of God, a man totally surrendered to God.

When he talks about departure, by the way, he is not talking about leaving the prison and getting back on the mission field or retiring back to his ancestral home in Tarsus. He is talking about his death. Paul is heading to his real home, at last.

In verse 7 he shows his understanding of what he has done:

I have fought the good fight, I have finished the race, I have kept the faith.

Here are three perfect tense verbs, with each showing finished action. It is over. I have fought the good fight. I did exactly what God sent me to do. I went where He sent me. I did what He told me to do. I said what he wanted me to say.

Some months ago, I had a remarkable experience that I will not forget for a long time. For two days Emma Lou and I had been in rural Ogun State, in Imalaland, in a small village. We had spent a peaceful day there in a spiritual retreat when we decided to pay a visit to His Royal Highness, the Kabiyesi of Imala. And as we left the palace of the Kabiyesi, driving back to our guest house, I suddenly had an impulse to ask the driver to stop the car and let me out so I could trek back.

As I stepped down from the vehicle and began walking down that village road, I suddenly had an incredible déjà vu experience. God gave me a flashback to something that happened around fifty years earlier. As a young 19-year-old, in June of 1967, I was in the hinterland of northwestern Mexico, in the foothills of the great Sierra Madre Occidental mountain chain, having the time of my life.

Perhaps in part my flashback was because the sights and sounds and even the smells in Mexico were similar to what I was experiencing that day in Imalaland. There in Mexico in 1967 I had already become fluent in Spanish. As a result, missionaries had invited me to Chihuahua State. There I was, far out in the bush, working in the fields by day and preaching to the villagers at night.

One day I told the villagers I would not be going to work. Instead I grabbed my .22 rifle and my Bible. I trekked out to a hilltop overlooking the village. There it was, as I spent several hours in prayer and the reading of scripture, that God unexpectedly showed up with a message that was to change my life forever. The message was a simple one: "This is your life. I want you to become a cross-cultural missionary." Even though God had already called me into the preaching ministry, I had not gone to Mexico with the expectation or idea that I would become a missionary. But God spoke to me, and the message was undeniably clear.

The memory of those long-ago happenings in Mexico is what came rushing back into my mind some months ago, there in Imala, Ogun State. It was as though God were saying to me, "It's me again. Welcome back! I'm the one who spoke to you on that hilltop in Mexico fifty years ago. You have now come full circle."

I am sure I was not yet where Paul is in these verses in 2 Timothy 4, but someday before terribly long I will get there. And that is the time I will be able to look back, like Paul. I am trusting God that I will be able to follow him in saying, "It's over. I have done it. I went where you told me to go. I did what you asked me to do. And I said what you wanted me to say."

That is why Paul expresses that great hope in verse 8 that I have mentioned. Something is in store for me. A crown of righteousness. Paul was an overcomer. There is nothing that can be more exciting than that, my dear reader: to go home at last, a complete victor.

For some people the coming of death or the return of Christ would represent the collapse and the end of their fondest dreams. Not so with Paul. I am talking of people who have worked all their lives to achieve that dream home, or that dream retirement, or that dream world tour, or whatever. Death, for them, would represent the end of the dream. But not so for Paul. As he put it so well earlier, *"For me to live is Christ, and to die is gain"* (Phil. 1:21).

But come with me as we finish this chapter together. Paul is not quite done yet. In the final fourteen verses he gives us what I believe is his great formula for how to grow old. I may not be able to unpack all he is saying here, but I will give at least get some of the high points.

The first important thing here is that Paul does not have a concept of retirement as we see it today. In modern times many of our cultures have almost deified the concept of retirement. They have idyllic dreams of spending the last twenty years of one's life in ease and comfort. Frankly, Paul would be appalled with that concept. Paul says, much to the contrary, that he wants death to interrupt his ministry. He clearly wants and expects to go all the way to the end in the harness for Jesus.

> *Be diligent to come to me quickly; for Demas has forsaken me, having loved this present world, and has departed for Thessalonica—Crescens for Galatia, Titus for Dalmatia. Only Luke is with me. Get Mark and bring him with you, for he is useful to me for ministry. And Tychicus I have sent to Ephesus. Bring the cloak that I left with Carpus at Troas when you come—and the books, especially the parchments.* (vv. 9-12)

What we can see here in these verses, even as Paul is sitting in prison, is that he has ministry fronts going on all around him in at least five different directions. He is a bit like Caleb in the Old Testament, who at eighty-five years of age told General Joshua, *"Give me this mountain. . . . My eye is not dimmed, and I am ready to keep pushing forward"* (Josh. 14:12).

Second, right up to the end Paul took care to surround himself with good people, including several life-long companions. It is true that some, like Demas, proved unfaithful, but Paul could still count on strong help from numerous people, including Timothy, Titus, Crescens and others. He was still carrying on a strong mentoring ministry and working hand in hand with other great people. The psalmist said: *"Now also when I am old and gray headed, O God, do not forsake me, until I declare Your strength to this generation, your power to everyone who is to come"* (Psalm 71:18). Paul was doing that.

Third, Paul wanted to go all the way to the end personally growing spiritually. He said in verse 13, *"Bring me especially the parchments."* He was referring to the scriptures. Bring my Bible. Let me grow old and die with the Bible in my hands. He was saying, I want to go all the way down to the end feeding myself every single day on the word of God.

Fourth (and maybe this one will surprise you) Paul says I want to be a hated man all the way to the end. I want someone here on this earth who will be glad to get the news when I take my flight to God's eternal home. I want to die with people somewhere who consider me their enemy. In verse 14 (right in the middle of this passage), he says:

> *Alexander the metalworker did me a great deal of harm. The Lord will repay him for what he has done.*

What happened? Paul had made a lot of enemies while he was in Ephesus, and some of them still would not forgive him. The workers in gold and silver and copper had ganged up on him because his preaching of Jesus was demolishing their business in idol-making and other occult paraphernalia. Paul was a man with a bounty on his head. I can assure you when Paul died there was rejoicing not just in heaven, but also in hell: "We are glad this man is gone forever from the face of the earth."

I am reminded of my good friend Dean Hostetler, a Mennonite layman from Nappanee, Indiana, whom I met in 1988 and who came to Nigeria in 1989 to help us conduct a seminar on demonic deliverance. Dean was an absolute terror to Satan because of his incredibly successful ministry in demonic deliverance, carried out over many years. That ministry extended all over Indiana, Ohio, Pennsylvania, and beyond, even right here in Nigeria. He often handled the toughest cases that others could not touch. As a result, I promise you that the halls of hell were relieved the day that godly man Dean Hostetler was carried into heaven by the holy angels.

Finally, Paul ends his message with a deep note of confidence that God will see him right through to the end and then take him home in peace and safety. Verse 18:

> *The Lord will rescue me from every evil attack and will bring me safely to his heavenly kingdom. To him be glory for ever and ever. Amen.*

WOW! There you have Paul's formula for growing old. It's in the Bible. I am sure many of my readers who are a lot younger than I are a million miles away in your thinking from what I am talking about, but be patient. You will get there! And when you do, look up what Paul is saying here.

Thank God for the life of Paul! And thank God for his godly instructions to Timothy.

Focus on Wesley Duewel

When I think about someone growing old with grace I think of my dear friend, Dr. Wesley Duewel, who went to be with the Lord just three months short of his 100th birthday, in 2016. He was raised in a very godly home and gave his life to God at a tender age. Eventually, he spent more than 70 years of his life invested in the cause of cross-cultural missions. Twenty-five years were spent in India. Later he served another twenty-five years as the president of the world-wide mission organization, the One Mission Society (OMS). The last twenty-five years were spent in a world-wide ministry of missions, prayer and writing.

Dr. Duewel was an author with a powerful pen. He wrote with dynamic unction on the Holy Spirit, revival, and soul winning, calling God's people back to prayer, the source of all power and passion for ministry. His hundreds of poems and all of his books express his hunger and passion. His articles have appeared in many publications. He edited the *Revival Magazine,* published in 12 languages.

His book *Touch the World through Prayer*, first published in 1986, is now in its 32nd printing. In 1987 I purchased

10,000 copies of that book, many of which were distributed around Nigeria. Later we published here in Nigeria around 50,000 copies of some of his later books, including *Ablaze for God*, *Mighty Prevailing Prayer*, *Revival Fire*, and *More God, More Power*. More than 2.5 million copies of his books are now in circulation in 58 languages or national editions around the world. International editions continue to be published, especially in India and China.

We had the honor of receiving Dr. Duewel in Nigeria for three national prayer conferences, in 1994. We started in Owerri, then moved to Kaduna, and finally to Ibadan. In subsequent years, I had the privilege of visiting Dr. Duewel nearly on an annual basis, until the final three years of his life. I shall never forget some of our times together as he would ask pointed questions about the progress of the work in Nigeria. I would never go away from his presence without a gift of more books, and always with the power of the prayers he offered for me, my wife, and the work of God in Africa.

Dr. Duewel was a man of scripture and a man of exemplary prayer. I can remember on several occasions in the 1990s hearing him say to me, "Gary, I pray for you every day." I cannot express how humbled and amazed I was to hear such words. Who was I anyway? Yet here was a man who had prayed for thousands of people over the years. He practiced what he preached. He was a humble man, but also a man focused on God, and focused on scripture and prayer.

I shall never forget something that happened when he and I were staying together at the Guest House at the University of Ibadan, while he was conducting daily prayer conferences at the Gospel Faith Mission Tabernacle. One morning he came to my room and asked if he could borrow a pencil. I did not have a pencil but asked him why he needed one. He said, "This morning I finished reading through the Old Testament. Every time I finish reading it, I make another pencil mark in the back of my Bible."

I could not resist asking him the follow-up question. "How many times have you read through the Old Testament?" He replied, "Today I finished the Old Testament for the 176th time." He then went on to say that for every time he read through the Old Testament, he normally read the New Testament twice. You would have to know Dr. Duewel to know that he was not saying any of that in a boastful manner. Heaven forbid. That was just who he was. A man of the scriptures!

Dr. Duewel finished well. The good news is that so can you and I. Praise be to God!

www.ingramcontent.com/pod-product-compliance
Lightning Source LLC
Chambersburg PA
CBHW070003180726
48002CB00019B/1892